Ellecia Clarke-Edwards

Two Kingdom Keys to Success

Mind Elevation + Spiritual Alertness

DAYELight
PUBLISHERS

ISBN: 978-1-949343-77-9

Elevate your mind! Become more spiritually aware and enjoy success in all areas of your life!

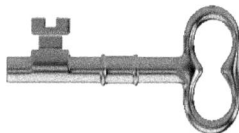

DEDICATION

This book is dedicated to all those who are in search of their God-given purpose on earth and are in a relentless pursuit to live a purpose-driven life.

This book is dedicated to persons who have a strong desire to be successful in ALL areas of life.

ACKNOWLEDGEMENT

I would like to thank God for His grace and mercies while writing this book.

I would also like to thank my husband, Gilbert Edwards, for his encouragement and support while writing.

Thank you to all my friends who expressed an interest by asking me about the book, which served as encouragement to finish.

Special thanks to my prayer partner, Brother Eaton McKoy, who was consistent in praying for me in getting this book completed.

I acknowledge and I am extremely grateful for my Pastor in Miami, Florida, Pastor Jose Olanso, for his profound teaching on deliverance, which significantly contributed to my spiritually elevated mindset.

TABLE OF CONTENT

PART ONE

MIND ELEVATION

PART TWO

SPIRITUAL ALERTNESS

INTRODUCTION

Your state of mind and your level of spiritual awareness/alertness will determine the overall success in all areas of your life.

Our lives require balance! Each area of our lives require attention for us to have that balance. What do I mean? There are different aspects of our lives: Spiritual, Physical, Financial, Emotional and Relationship. Majority of the time, your ability to spread your energy over the different areas of your life is limited to what is happening in one area. It requires extreme self–awareness and an intentional effort to balance one's life. Significant to the process of balancing is the condition of your spirit and mind.

This book does not represent any extensive research on the mind and the complexities thereof. However, what I can say is that my experiences have allowed me to draw the conclusion that there is a direct correlation between the condition of the spirit, the mind and one's ability to enjoy success in the different areas of life.

PART ONE of this book speaks about the power that an elevated mindset can have over the different areas of our lives. The fact is, one will never begin to walk in their true potential unless their mindset is elevated. An elevated mindset is one that wants to crush the neck of mediocrity beneath its feet; it wants to move from ordinary to extraordinary and will stop at nothing to get there. If you get to a point of saying, "I have had it with how I am living my life"; and you begin to change the way you think and act, then your mindset will begin to be elevated. Are you at a place where you are thinking, "I need a change from this situation?" If you have been saying this for a while, yet you have not done anything about it, your mindset has not yet been elevated. When an individual's mindset is elevated, they "take action."

PART TWO of this book speaks of spiritual alertness and the significance thereof. Being spiritually alert means being self-aware, being sober-minded, being watchful (See 1 Peter 5:8). Self-monitoring and self-examination are very important exercises. It is quite intrinsic for you to understand yourself: know what you are capable of doing and what is out of character.

A spiritually alert person will know when the enemy is messing around with their mind and is causing them to behave out of character. A self-aware, sober-minded person will know when there is an open door for demonic invasion in his or her life and will take the necessary steps to correct the out of character behavior through repentance. Proverbs 28:13 says: *"He that covereth his sins shall not prosper but whoso confesseth and forsaketh them shall have mercy."*

To be spiritually alert means to be conscious daily of where you stand in your relationship with the Lord. A spiritually alert person will know when they are deviating from their God-given principles on their Christian journey. The spiritually alert person is not afraid to admit it when they have gone off course on a tangent; they then take the necessary steps to pull themselves on course quickly. A spiritually alert individual can discern when there is a demonic spirit influencing their lives. The spirit of anger, rejection, lust, bitterness, among many others, are some demonic spirits mentioned in this book.

It is my prayer that God opens your spiritual eyes, and your mindset will be shifted as you read this book: for a life-changing experience.

PART ONE

MIND ELEVATION

CHAPTER 1
AN ELEVATED MINDSET

LAYING THE FOUNDATION

Humanity is in a desperate search for purpose. Most human beings have an innate need to self-manifest (discovering who they were truly born to be). Some people live a very casual life, some a mediocre life and others a poverty-stricken life. Essentially a lot of people simply tolerate life until an unfulfilled feeling dominates them. It is this feeling that initiates within them the pursuit for a "wow" moment, when they walk into an "elevated space"; one with a sense of purpose and they begin to want more than the mediocre. This space is what I call, "An Elevated Mindset"

WHAT IS AN ELEVATED MINDSET?

An elevated mindset is one that operates with a hunger to fulfil divine purpose. An elevated mind operates at a 'higher level of frequency'; always seeking to tune in to the Creator's agenda for its being. This mind constantly questions the vision behind action and reason behind the existence of objects and events. It is one that goes into a relentless search for purpose.

An elevated mindset often asks questions such as:

- Who am I?
- What was I created to do and to be?
- Why am I not living in the abundance that God has promised me through His Word?
- Why am I in a constant place of poverty?
- Why are opportunities passing me by?
- Why am I not walking in my purpose?
- Why am I in fear and not walking in my God-given boldness?

When you seek answers to these deep questions, it means you are now thinking at a higher level. It is time for you to operate at that high level. What do I mean? To think about something is one thing but operating in it is quite another. Someone with a completely elevated mindset will not stop at the imagination of something great; this person will take action towards their thought. In other words, they execute what they contemplate.

An elevated mindset is what pulls you from a seated position to a standing position; it makes comfort zones uncomfortable; It converts a "talker" into a "doer." An elevated mindset will pull you out of complacency into competence and reliability. An elevated mindset is one that will say, "I am responsible for my own life; I will not leave the fate of my destiny in someone else's hands." The elevated mindset is one that will say, "Where I am in this life is because of the decisions I made" (holding yourself fully accountable). You will not entertain the blame game, if you have an elevated mindset. Once you begin operating with this kind of mindset, then you will begin to experience greater order in your life. You will begin to operate with a sense of purpose and urgency.

CONTROL YOUR THOUGHTS

The mind is a powerful tool that still eludes man's full comprehension. We are powerful beings that have the potential to do anything we set our minds to accomplish. Our minds can be our greatest friend; but it can also be our worst enemy.

The things that happen in life do not "just happen." Things that happen in life are a direct result of mindset (your thoughts), which leads to choices. As you are reading this book, wherever you are

21

right now, there is something that is dominating your thoughts. Your decision arising from your thought-pattern can either be positive or negative and will have repercussions, which can either be good or bad. Whatever thoughts you pondered on in the past, created the present moment you are in right now. This is a reality that many people may not readily admit.

As a ripple effect from the actions of our forefather, Adam, we are wired to blame our circumstances for our challenges. We find it easier to point a finger at others for our current situation. These blame games are often the cause of our downfall; we do not take responsibility for our own choices and, therefore, end up not making due changes within ourselves to set a course for success. Being Adam's descendants, there are two 'convenient' yet destructive games we inherited from our fore-parents:

1. The Victim Game
2. The Blame Game

THE VICTIM GAME

The victim game is for procrastinators who are addicted to pity. They feel sorry for themselves in just about any circumstance. Self-pity is a time bandit; I have seen self-pity steal decades of people's lives. A person with victim mentality blames everybody else but themselves for the circumstances they are in. They always have a sad story behind their procrastination and under-achieved life. They burden others with the fate of their experiences and their destinies. They always want others around them to sooth the wounds of their long gone past or the sores presented by today's challenges. They are not solution seekers; rather, they are selfish people who are too proud to get their hands dirty in finding a solution for their problems. We all know this saying, "misery loves company." There are always those people in your life who are feeling sorry for themselves, thinking that life is crueler to them than it is to anyone else. A victim-minded person forgets that there is no trouble that is not common to man. They take their trouble, own it, and even nurture it with the hope that someone will take up the burden of trying to soothe them. Victim mentality is a dangerous and wicked addiction.

I charge you today to take stock of your networks and identify such people in your life. You must tell them, "No more pity party over here." You must begin to cut these people out of your personal space as soon as possible. Fellowship with them is an obstacle to your destiny, rather than a link to your success. They are toxic to your energy. If you must engage them, do it from a distance. If you are one of them, flee from the pity party before more of your time and destiny slips through your hands.

THE BLAME GAME

In this game, the player perceives himself or herself as always being perfect. You will often hear a blamer uttering self-vindicating statements such as "it's not my fault." The blame game is very popular because it puts the player in the 'perfect' zone, while convicting everybody else. It is addictive because it creates a false sense of peace within your mind; even our fore-parents, Adam and Eve, could not resist it (See Genesis 3). Isn't it funny that when they were each making up their mind to sin, they did not consult anybody, but suddenly their actions became somebody else's fault?

The blame game will rob you of precious time and opportunity for growth; the kind of growth that comes through self-correction and self-evaluation.

You must end the games today and take charge of your mental state. It is time for you to get in the driver's seat of your destiny and steer your way to a successful life.

This is not to say that I downplay the unfortunate circumstances that could have taken place in your life, that were beyond your control. What I am saying is, these circumstances may have been the forces that steered you off destiny's course, but at some point in life it will be up to you to acknowledge your pain, the effects of the trauma on you and seek the spiritual help necessary to bring your life back on course. It will not be easy, but it is worth it. Seek the help of God and those He has placed in your life to hold your hand through such times as these. Make a deliberate resolve to take back the wheel to steer your life back on course. For example, being sexually, emotionally or physically abused as a child is a traumatic experience that had nothing to do with your decisions or actions. It is not your fault; blame game and victim game are not applicable in a scenario of this nature, because you were truly a victim. This trauma will take you through a myriad of feelings you cannot control, for example, anger, resentment, bitterness, etc. Demonic spirits work full-force and overtime in such a situation, to keep you in bondage. It will take much more than will power to overcome. More of this will be discussed in Part Two of this book. It is important to seek spiritual help in such circumstances. You will need prayer, deliverance, continued consecration and spiritual alertness and continuous counselling to keep these spirits out.

TAKE 100% RESPONSIBILITY

Taking responsibility means being accountable. This requires a certain level of awareness and consciousness. It also requires a certain level of maturity. You must hold yourself accountable for both your successes and your failures. Too often we go through life taking the credit for the successes we experience, but we blame our failures on others and circumstances. The time has come for you to look yourself in the mirror, be honest with yourself and accept the hard truth that the things that did not work out as expected require responsibility and solution; not the victim and the blame game. Take 100% responsibility for where you are; it is the first step to changing where you are.

SELF-LIMITING BELIEF

Self-limiting belief aids the blame and victim game in keeping success at bay. What are self-limiting beliefs? It is a negative or underestimating perception about oneself, that one accepts to be true. Self-limiting beliefs are serious hindrances to the manifestation of one's purpose/goals. These beliefs are driven by fear rather than faith, which results in procrastination. The good news is that this self-limiting belief can be changed to self-empowering thinking. To do this, you must first understand that a belief is just a thought or a combination of thoughts, which are conceived of external words, events or cultures; it is not necessarily the reality. You need to change your thoughts from self-limiting to self-empowering thoughts.

Who are you? What have you accepted to be true about yourself? As you read this book, there are so many things that you want to do but you are procrastinating, because you believe you are not good enough or powerful enough to get it done. That ends today. Those limiting thoughts end today. Look yourself in the mirror every day and tell yourself that you are important, powerful and competent through Christ Jesus. You can do all things through Christ who strengthens you. Repeat this every day; repetitions are powerful and ultimately affect your mindset. That excellent business idea you have, pursue it. That book you want to write, write it. All you need to do is start.

Stop playing it safe and begin to live your life. If you fail, so what? Get up and go again. I have failed many times and I have come to understand, if not through experience then through observation, that a regretful life is a sorrowful and impactless life. You do not want to get up one day and realize you are at an age of regret; a time when you look back and start saying "I wish" or "I should have." By that time, it may be too late. Mr. John Maxwell's book speaks about Failing Forward. Recognize that there are lessons in failure, learn from them, grow from them, and move on; do not fail to try.

Self-limiting beliefs are fear-driven and inhibit faith. Inhibited faith is one of the parents of procrastination, and procrastination results in stagnation.

The following chart illustrates the vicious cycle of self-limiting belief.

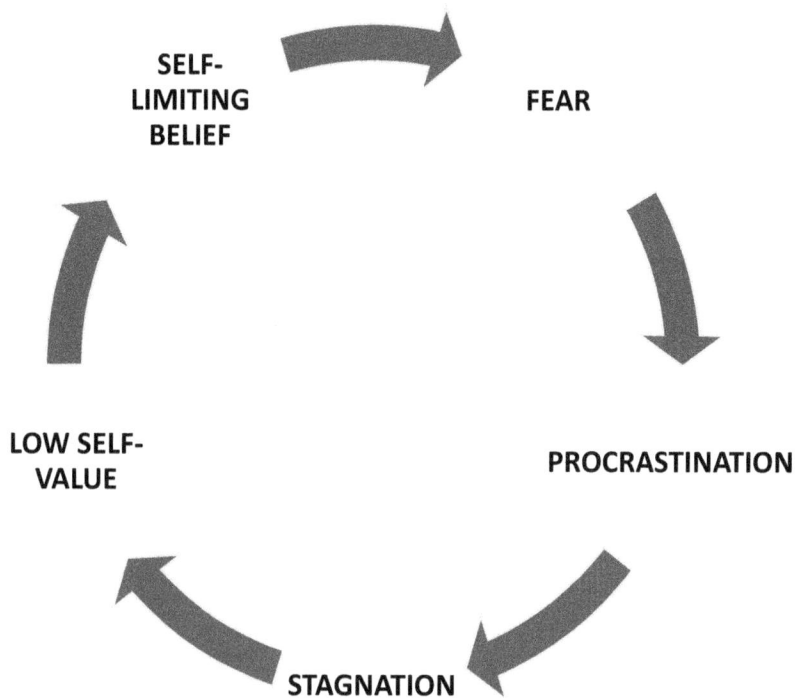

CHAPTER 2
A MADE-UP MIND: PURPOSE/GOALS

A made-up mind is a powerful result of finding purpose, a powerful force driving this purpose, and a powerful force in achieving purpose. What is purpose? Purpose, in this context, is simply God's agenda for your presence on earth, in service to His kingdom and humanity. Each passing day of not living in your purpose is a wasted day. Time lost cannot be regained. The question is, what is your purpose? What is that God-given thing that you were created to achieve? Are you actively pursuing it? Actively pursuing your God-given purpose means spending some good quality time and energy to advance towards it every day. When I started writing this book, I spent at least two hours daily working on it because I received direct instructions from the Holy Spirit to write it. The very name came to me as I meditated on the goodness of the Lord in my life. The Lord eventually revealed to me that writing this book was part of my ministerial calling. As I pursued the completion of this book, I certainly had my fair share of fear, procrastination and stagnation. I had to press forth towards the goal of releasing this book. I felt the flame of my sense of purpose burning at a higher intensity in my belly.

You may ask yourself, "How do I know what my purpose is?" Well, I will tell you how. The Bible says: "Ask and it shall be given to you; seek and ye shall find; knock and it shall be opened unto you" (Matthew 7:7). Asking God is the first step to finding your purpose because as your Creator, He designed you uniquely and knitted you in your mother's womb with a specific agenda in mind for you. The question is, "Have you actually asked the Lord through prayer?" The Bible says: "Be careful for nothing; but in every thing by prayer and supplication with thanksgiving let your requests be made known unto God." (Philippians 4:6). When I became very desperate to understand my purpose and calling, this Scripture solidified my reason for the need to go into deep fasting and prayer. If you lack the wisdom of understanding your purpose, go to God today and ask Him to reveal it to you.

"If any man lacks wisdom, let him ask God, that giveth to all men liberally and upbraideth not and it shall be given him." (James 1:5).

How Does A Made-Up Mind Drive Achievement of Purpose?

I believe that man is consistently in search of something. Some believe that if they got married, became millionaires or had children, all would be well. These are wonderful things to achieve, but they are not your purpose for existence; they may simply propel you to achieving your purpose. You must therefore have your divine purpose in sight. While money, children, career, property and others such as these are important, getting hung up on these will make you fail to identify your true value to God's agenda for His Kingdom and for humanity. Let's say, for instance, you have acquired all of these things, what next? These things need to serve your pursuit of divine purpose; beside this, they are reduced to vanities of life. It is sad that the world measures up success to the neighbourhood of your mansion, car model, number of children, career and such achievements. Achievement of one's divine purpose in service to humanity is often overlooked in the absence of such achievements. I charge you to look around. Wealthy and famous men with the so-called perfect family and all the wealth in the world are committing suicide.

Doing a diligent search to discover what you were created to become is one of the most prudent actions you could ever take in life.

If you are not manifesting your divine purpose, you will ultimately feel unfulfilled. There may be temporary fixes; however, ultimately, you will not experience the kind of lasting joy and contentment that only comes with fulfilling God's purpose for your life. One of man's deepest fear is to die with regrets: the regret of living an unfulfilled life; the regret of dying without manifesting purpose.

Once you have asked the Lord to reveal what your purpose is, and you are now in the know, it is time to make up your mind to fulfill your purpose. A made-up mind is a strong inner desire or intention to get something done or to act in a certain manner. You will never get anything done unless your mind is made up. A person who has made up their mind is one who has made a decision on a matter and will not change their stand in the face of different circumstances, even unfavourable circumstances. There are two main qualities that are a manifestation of a made-up mind:

1. Discipline

A made-up mind translates to having the discipline to getting that thing done. To be disciplined means to have the ability to persevere no matter what. When you have a made-up mind to get a goal accomplished, you will stick to it no matter what. When you have the privilege of knowing what your purpose is and making up your mind to accomplish it no matter what, you are at a powerful place in your life.

32

2. Focus

Focus can only exist in the presence of vision, which is birthed out of knowing one's divine purpose. It involves keeping your time and energy fixated on a vision, therefore steering all tasks at hand to serve the vision. To a focused mind, things may arise, but they remain insignificant until the mission is accomplished, and the vision is tangible.

Avoid sharing your vision goals and ideas with too many people. Sharing your ideas with too many people and unnecessarily soliciting their opinion and admiration is a sure diversion from destiny's path. So, you may reason: "The more ideas and opinions I seek and consider, the better the decision I will make." However, let me emphasize this: it is very bad idea. With many assistance also come many haters, whose sole reason for engaging you is to make sure that you succeed at nothing. Stay vigilant in your engagements; keep your networks lean and "clean." Trying to get your mind made up in a vast myriad of ideas and opinions will lead to confusion and, eventually, procrastination due to indecision.

It is also important to identify the "yes" people in your life; the ones who agree with you in everything, good or bad. They do not have an opinion of their own, and even if they do, they will not express it. Such will agree with you with an agenda to please you, either out of fear or out of deceit. Such people are an impediment to your vision.

In 1 Kings 22, King Jehosophat was wise enough to discern the "yes" prophets. He rejected their pleasing but deceitful counsel. He sought instruction from a true prophet of God, Micaiah, despite the discomfort of hearing unpleasant truth. He understood that only true counsel can preserve his kingdom and his life, even if it came from a prophet who always prophesied doom upon him. He was not interested in engaging in deceitful pleasant chats; the fate of his kingdom and his life was at stake. Likewise, the fate of your destiny and those around you is at stake. Seek the right counsel, even when it is uncomfortable. You must get rid of "yes" people around you to create room for level-headed people, who are not afraid to shine light on any of the occasional nonsense that impedes your progress.

LACK OF KNOWLEDGE AFFECTS THE MANIFESTATION OF PURPOSE/GOALS

It is said that knowledge is power; the more you know, the more you can achieve. Ignorance, on the other hand, is one of the greatest enemies of success. When I started my personal exploration of the "Mind Research" I had many "wow" moments. Soon after, I started to kick myself, figuratively, for not being aware of the information I came across. I am no expert on the subject of the mind. However, I have taken the time to learn enough and use the information garnered to bring about manifestations of great potentials.

The manifestations I have experienced came through a strong desire to understand how our brain/mind works. Garnering this knowledge has undoubtedly elevated my position of authority in the subject. For example, I now understand that my mind can talk me out of getting something done. When I started to write this book, my mind would tell me "Ellecia, you are not a writer. What do you think you are doing?" This created doubt in my mind about my ability to complete this book. However, my thought pattern shifted when I discovered, through research, how powerful "affirmations" are. The mind aligns to your affirmations. Your actions, which are a manifestation of the instruction in your mind, become aligned to your affirmations as well. I continued to tell myself that I will complete this book. My affirmations continued daily, and I sought the Lord's help. He instructed me directly through His Word and through the guidance of the Holy Spirit. Other times, He would send people my way to support the course. The end result is obvious, you are reading the book.

What has your mind talked you out of doing? Did you want to give a motivational speech and your mind told you that you are not bold enough? Did you want to start your own business only for your mind to convince you that you do not have what it takes? Did you stop yourself from getting information on how to obtain the house you desire simply because your mind told you that you can never afford it? Did you stop on the track of upgrading your car because your mind told you, "Look here, you should be happy you even have a car. Just settle for your 10-year-old car. You are just fine." I speak about these particular points because I can testify to all these circumstances. My mind held me back for years with all these negatives. Over time, I achieved all of the above by shutting down the self-limiting voice in my head.

KNOWLEDGE IS POWER: POWER FORMULA FOR SUCCESS

When I changed how I read the Bible and started to truly meditate on God's promises; when I coupled this with my research on the power of the mind, my mindset shifted. I began to take bolder steps. I gave my first speech as a "Keynote Speaker" at my company's

Strategic Meeting. After that session, a number of people approached me to congratulate me and to express how much the speech motivated them. Some of them posited, "I am full of life and energy going into this new year, after that speech." The CEO of the company said, "I was moved by your speech." I drove home full of excitement that evening. I was so excited that I could hardly eat. For years, I shied away from public speaking engagements; my mind had convinced me that I could not do it. I had to work hard at nullifying that negative voice and began to affirm myself that I can do it. I charge you to shut up that negative voice in your mind today.

Through continued reading of the Word of God, and research, I realized my own personal formula for success. This formula was tested and proven repeatedly. I manifested my success through **prayer, a made-up mind, and faith-driven action**. Note my formula below:

PRAYER+ A MADE-UP MIND+ FAITH -DRIVEN ACTION= SUCCESS

```
                    PRAYER


                   SUCCESS

   A MADE                        FAITH-
     UP                          DRIVEN
    MIND                         ACTION
```

I grew up seeing my mother relocating at least six times by the time I finished high school. I therefore knew from a very early age that I needed to own my own home. It was my number one priority. After working at the bank for over five years, I started the process by gathering all the information necessary for purchasing a house.

I don't know about you, but I believe there are angels here on earth. The Word of God says: "Declaring the end from the beginning, and from ancient times the things that are not yet done, saying, My counsel shall stand, and I will do all my pleasures." (Isaiah 46:10). Therefore, God knows what you need before you even think about it. He sees the future; He knows the perfect time to send helpers your way. I can testify to this with the experience I had purchasing my house. My friend was like an angel on earth, sent at the perfect time to break a curse over my family line; the curse of 'not owning anything.'

When my dear friend and I drove to a certain part of St. Catherine, Jamaica, just merely eye shopping for a house, I came upon the house that I desired. We went into the model unit and I immediately felt a fire light up inside me. At that time, I was residing in Kingston and was working very closely to where I resided. I knew that venturing outside of the Kingston region would undoubtedly cost me travel time and money.

The fire that lit up inside me did not get quenched. I took several brochures that day. I laid them out on my bed that very evening and looked at them; I looked again, then I looked some more. The fire was blazing in my heart, but my mind kept talking against my faith. It told me that I was not in a position to buy the house; it told me that I could not dare accomplish this since nobody in my family ever owned a home. I had to work hard at shutting down those self-defeating thoughts.

THE USE OF MY SUCCESS FORMULA

After sleeping and dreaming of this house, I began to tell myself things like, "I have to purchase this house. This house is mine. I call this house to me now. I am already living in this house." By this time, my mind was made up *(formula: a made-up mind).* At that time, I had no idea how I was going to do it. I had no money saved up; I had no help from family, but I knew I wanted that house. I started to pray *(formula: prayer).* I believed the Word that says everything comes through prayer and supplication (See Philippians 4:6-7). When I looked at the current situation, I could do nothing else but pray. I started to save as much as I could from my salary as a Customer Service Representative at the bank. I cut my expenses radically and, for the first time, made a budget for each month *(formula: action).* Over a 3-month period, I found myself with $300,000 Jamaican dollars.

While I was saving, I amped up preparation for my house by starting to gather the necessary documentations, talking to the relevant agencies and gathering information about home ownership *(formula: taking action).* As my friend and I continued to talk about the house daily, I visualized myself in the house. I looked at the brochures daily; I prayed daily; I declared daily; I gathered information daily. Essentially, I kept the dream alive daily by conditioning my mind to believe that the house was already mine. My mind had no choice but to align to the determination of my faith.

SUCCESS FORMULA AT WORK

It was a little over three months of planning, praying and dreaming when my friend asked me, "How much money do you have saved up?" I said, "Almost $400,000." He then asked, "How much is the deposit?" I said, "$650,000." I have never forgotten what I felt when those four words came out of his mouth: "I will help you." He loaned me the remaining balance to help me beat the deadline for the sale of the house. He allowed me to pay him back monthly. I was super excited and moved into further action. By this time, I had all the information necessary to execute my vision. I initiated conversation with one of the Loans Officer at the branch and the rest is history.

My God-given opportunity was met, perhaps even inspired by my relentless preparation to acquire what my faith said I could have.

Please take note of the following instructions and statements and re-read them as many times as possible:

1. ***You cannot accomplish your goals by yourself***; you need other people. Through prayer, God will always send your helpers.

2. ***Faith without works is foolishness***. You cannot pray and sit down. You must move according to your faith and make its fruit manifest.

3. ***Do not park your goals after writing them down***. Look at them every day, declare and decree they will come to pass.

4. ***Wake up every day visualizing what it will feel like accomplishing your goals.***

I made-up my mind to own a house, I prayed daily about it and I took action. Five months later, I was in my own home. *(END RESULT: success).*

My mind caused a great delay in the acquisition of my home. I can remember looking at homes many other times prior to then and my mind was doing a number on me. My mind told me, "Why are you wasting your time? You know nobody owns a home in your family. It is impossible. Just leave it alone. You know you cannot afford it." It was not until I began to exercise the formula: PRAYER+A MADE-UP MIND+FAITH-BASED ACTION, that I manifested my home.

I manifested a new car and started my business using the same formula. Ignorance is no excuse. The accomplishment of your goals is fully up to you. It is easy to talk about what we want to do; it is easy to write down what you want to do. However, unless you have a made-up mind, backed up with prayer and faith-based action, it will just remain on paper and never be accomplished.

I urge you to give this formula a try.

How Does One Get A "Made Up" Mind?

Earlier I suggested to you that a made-up mind must be backed by being disciplined and remaining focused. You may be saying, "Yep, easier said than done. I have made up my mind to do many things and it still does not get done." So, how does one actually get to that point?

The answer to this is simple: you need to be "sick and tired." Yes, all it takes to have a made-up mind is to be "sick and tired" of your current situation. My definition of being sick and tired means to be frustrated and desperate for change. Many people mistake this kind of ambition for greed and lack of contentment; it is, however, very different. Ambition acknowledges and appreciates present situation, examines the situation to see what can be better, then works towards the better version of life. When you look at your past circumstances, do you realize that you made up your mind because you felt frustrated or desperate or, plainly put, sick and tired of what was happening in your life? Go back in time, you will discover that I am right. I dare you to be ambitious.

Until you feel sick and tired of living a mediocre and purposeless life, you will not "make up your mind" to start moving in search of purpose. Unless you feel sick and tired of going to the doctor because of the illness that you are facing, you will not have a "made up mind' to start eating healthier and exercising at least three times per week. Unless you become sick and tired of hanging around negative people who do nothing but drain your energy, you will not have a "made up mind" to cut them out of your life and start attracting people who can propel you forward to your divine destiny. Unless you become sick and tired of your spouse physically and emotionally abusing you, you will not have a "made up mind" to end the toxic relationship.

You must be "fed-up"; "sick and tired", in order to change your current state of mind. The question is, what are you "sick and tired" of right now, as you are reading this book? Whatever it is, make up your mind to change your situation today. A change is a decision away; it does not take a minute. Stop procrastinating on that life-changing decision. The Lord asked me to write this book at this time and season, so you could read it and for the renewal of your mind right now. Your life depends on it, your ministry depends on it, your purpose depends on it, your prosperity depends on it, your children's future depends on it.

Your happiness depends on you, nobody else but you. Whatever you want to accomplish is up to you. PRAY + MAKE UP YOUR MIND + TAKE FAITH-BASED ACTION today. Resist the temptation to play the blame game and the victim game.

CHAPTER 3
SPIRITUAL TRANSFORMATION THROUGH MIND ELEVATION

A human being lives in three components: body (tangible physical aspect), soul (commonly referred to as heart or mind, where thoughts ideas and feelings are birthed) and spirit (often referred to as the "inner man", which is the breath of God within us, which causes us to inherit His nature and be in fellowship with Him). The body and mind together make up what the Bible often refers to: "the flesh" (See 1 Thessalonians 5:23). All these components are important for life and purpose. However, it is my belief that the Spirit bears more weight with regard to the wellbeing of your life, compared to the other components. In order to live a meaningful life, you must be able to identify with the Creator (our Maker). Regardless of what our day to day looks like, it is God's principles that govern the outcome of your action. For instance, the principle of seed and harvest is a Biblical principle. God designed the earth in such a manner that every seed gives birth to its own kind. You cannot harvest cashew nuts from the coconut tree you planted.

A life hooked up with our heavenly Father and an elevated mind focused on the true and pure things of God (See Philippians 4:8), will bring forth great success in just about anything you set out to do. The fact is, unless you pull your mind from the place of mediocrity and begin to focus on what God's Word has promised you, you will never become transformed into who you were created to be.

My experience with spiritual transformation started when I went into a deeper search of my God-given purpose. I went in deep prayer and fasting for one month and something radical took place.

THE BEGINNING OF MY JOURNEY

I worked at one of the most prestigious banks in Jamaica for over ten years. I had embarked on my banking career in Telling, and I had a string of promotions. I worked my way up from Teller to part-time Customer Service Representative (CSR), and from there to a full-time CSR position. I supervised the CSR until I was eventually promoted to the Business Banking Department. My goal was to become a Bank Manager. However, in the process of pursuing my achievements, I realized that I no longer desired the career I worked so long to have.

I embarked on a search for my purpose. Through prayer and fasting, my eyes were opened. I soon realized that the desire of my heart to go into Branch Management was not aligned with God's desire for me. Over time, I felt unfulfilled in my job; I felt empty; I felt that there was something bigger, something greater for me to do. On one hand I thought, "I have a steady job that provided me with pension, health coverage and day to day expense security. There's no need to make big changes right now." On the other hand, there was such a strong discomfort that indicated to my spirit that my time in the banking sector was up. My spirit desired to be aligned with God's will for me; while my soul and body wanted to continue basking in my career achievements, which were admirable to many. My flesh and my spirit wrestled. I asked the Lord for clarity and to help me make up my mind.

The back and forth reasoning in my mind continued for over six months. In February 2017, I took my vacation and decided to travel for the first time. My intended vacation time was three weeks.

However, the Lord had something different in mind. I did not know that when I boarded that plane, I was going on a spiritual journey.

SHIFTED CHRISTIAN EXPERIENCE

I continued in deep prayer and fasting while attending a ministry that my then fiancé was attending in Miami, Florida. Attending that ministry was the beginning of my spiritual mindset transformation. I started to learn some mind-changing things that shifted my entire Christian journey. My level of thinking concerning the things of the Spirit was radically shifted. My mindset was elevated to another level due to my experiences.

This was a deliverance ministry, very different from what I was accustomed to in Jamaica. It was a refreshing change; I had never been exposed to this aspect of ministry before. I became very intrigued by deliverance ministry. I started to do extensive research on it. As I went deeper into this knowledge, the Lord spoke to me about the serious lack that exist in today's church in this area (deliverance). The Bible says: "Heal the sick, cleanse the lepers, raise the dead, cast out devils…." (Matthew 10:8). Why are we not witnessing and taking part in the manifestation of these in the churches? The works of the Holy Spirit have become such rare occurrences that they raise suspicion and scrutiny, even among church members, on the rare occasions they do happen. Many still operate as bound Christians.

When the Lord revealed these things to me, my mindset shifted concerning the body of Christ. No longer was I thinking about my own Christian journey, but the journey of my brothers and sisters who were oppressed by demonic spirits and needed deliverance.

I witnessed many events of deliverance in this ministry and my heart broke because, for the first time, I understood what it meant to be oppressed by the enemy and not knowing that you are oppressed. I saw my fellow brothers and sisters in Christ with serious purpose over them, held back in demonic oppression and bondage. I realized then that this was such a significant and well needed area of ministry in all churches; not some, ALL.

I saw demonic spirits manifest in so many forms. I witnessed demons talking and crumbling under the presence of God. In one service, the demon in a young lady said, "You are causing chaos to my kingdom." As two strong gentlemen in the church held on to this young lady, she kept backing away from the Pastor toward the wall, until her legs climbed the wall in a backward motion. The demon said, "I can't stand the light that is inside you", as the Pastor continued with the deliverance session.

One Thursday night, the glory of God was so strong during deliverance that a young lady attempted to run through the door. Two strong men in the ministry held on to her. The Pastor exclaimed, "Let her go" and proceeded to say, "Angels of my Father, I ask you to bind her right hand behind her." In that instance, I saw with my own two eyes: she struggled as the angels bound her hand behind her. I didn't see the angel, but I witnessed her trying hard to resist her hand being pulled behind her. The Pastor continued by saying, "Angel of my Father, I ask you to bind her left hand behind her." I witnessed the same occurrence. I witnessed that young lady standing there still. She could not move until the end of the deliverance proceedings.

At the end, the Pastor exclaimed, "Release her angels of my Father. I thank you." The Pastor then took her through deliverance, and she was freed. I literally broke down in that service at the awesome power of God.

Of course, this completely blew my mind. I had seen instances of deliverance before, but certainly not to that magnitude. I cried at the end of many of these sessions. It was then that I realized that so many people are oppressed, depressed and suppressed. The fact is, unless they go through "deliverance," they will not be free. This is undoubtedly lacking in the body of Christ. There are many who are going through challenges right now and they believe it is normal. They take it for granted, thinking that it is just "life happening." Many are sick, many are in poverty and many are facing misfortune one after another. In many of these circumstances, demonic forces are at work and deliverance is mandatory to be fully free.

Over time, I developed a passion for deliverance. I believed that the people of God must be free from demonic oppression. The Lord then placed on my heart a burden to do a deliverance manual on spirits and how they manifest. This came out of a hunger and a desperate desire to see God's people set free. It became a passion of mine to complete this manual and make it available to as many churches as possible, so that the body of Christ can be edified in this respect. This desire is what forms Part Two of this book.

So, there I was in another country, locked away in prayer and fasting, away from my family, friends and regular routine. I was attending this new ministry, under which I was learning how to handle the matter of deliverance. It was in this space and time, in that season, that my spirit man shifted to another level. It was through this ministry that I gained a better understanding of the significance of "watching our thoughts." Thoughts of anger, jealousy, resentment, bitterness are all spirits; once entertained in your mind, you will begin to manifest them over time (See more in Part Two).

I pause here to say that when you are in search of your purpose, you must be ready to step into unfamiliar territory, pull yourself away from the regular and be ready to become uncomfortable. Change is often uncomfortable because we are wired to do the norm and any deviation from the norm registers in our minds as a problem at the first instant. In addition to this, the enemy does not want you to be in the know, he does not want you to walk in your purpose. Most importantly, he does not want your mind to be elevated to a more mature conscious place. He therefore convinces you that the uncomfortable change is unnecessary, and that you are fine just as you are. He may even deceive you into thinking that your situation is according to "fate" and "destiny" and that it will never change for the better.

EFFECT OF RIGHT THINKING ON YOUR SPIRITUAL JOURNEY

Right thinking is harnessing pure and beneficial thoughts. Your spirit man is the central core of your being. If you are spiritually impoverished, it significantly impacts all other areas of your life. If you do not spend time with the Lord, and understand what He wants you to do, you will wander through life without aim.

The outcome of everything you do depends on the condition of your mindset. If your mind is entertaining negative thoughts, it will attract demonic forces into your atmosphere to contaminate your spirit. The maintenance of pure thoughts is very important to the health of your spirit. Pure thoughts will keep your spirit in the presence of God and, therefore, keep unclean thoughts from penetrating your mind. The enemy will always seek to attack your mind. Once he penetrates your mind, he can shut down your body through a spirit of lethargy. This spirit will steal your joy and your zest for life.

There is no doubt that we are on a battlefield. You are blessed if your mind is stayed on the Lord. 2 Corinthians 11:3 says that the thought of believers can be corrupted. Hence, it is very important to guard your mind from the fiery darts of the enemy. You must guard your mind from impure thoughts lest you open the door for demonic forces to contaminate your spirit man.

The more we continue on our Christian journey, the fiercer attacks on our minds will be. God's protection comes through prayer and meditation on the Word of God. The Bible says, "Pray without ceasing" (See 1 Thessalonians 5:17). When you arise in the morning, you need to ask the Lord for His full armor.

Put on the whole armour of God, that ye may be able to stand against the wiles of the devil. For we wrestle not against flesh and blood, but against principalities, against powers, against the rulers of the darkness of this world, against spiritual wickedness in high places. Wherefore take unto you the whole armour of God, that ye may be able to withstand in the evil day, and having done all, to stand. Stand therefore, having your loins girt about with truth, and having on the breastplate of righteousness; and your feet shod with the preparation of the gospel of peace; above all, taking the shield of faith, wherewith ye shall be able to quench all the fiery darts of the wicked. And take the helmet of salvation, and the sword of the Spirit, which is the word of God: praying always with all prayer and supplication in the Spirit, and watching thereunto with all perseverance and supplication for all saints. (Ephesians 6:11-18).

This Scripture emphasizes the significance of prayer as the only way we can protect our mind from evil thoughts. Even believers who are very faithful to the Lord cannot withstand the attacks, if they are exposed to the influence of worldly standards. The shield of faith quenches all the flaming darts, and the helmet of salvation keeps away all the negative thoughts. We need this covering.

In a world filled with so many distractions, it sometimes becomes very difficult to not be drawn away by negativity. In fact, most of what we see around us are negative. It therefore requires being alert and sensitive to the Holy Spirit to counter these negative influences. The Word of God says that the enemy goes around like a roaring lion seeking those he may devour (See 1 Peter 5:8). He is consistently looking for a way to pull us away from the Lord and to pull us out of God's presence.

BECOME SELF AWARE

It is very important to be self-aware and walk in that high sense of consciousness. This will require practice. You must monitor your thoughts in such a way that you know exactly when a negative thought pops up. When you recognize this happening, call it out. Calling out a negative thought means acknowledging that you are experiencing a negative thought. At this point, through self-awareness, you get the opportunity to replace that negative thought with a positive thought. Is this easy? Absolutely not! This requires being in tune with self and being extremely self-aware. Dr. Caroline Leaf speaks about the negative effect of a negative thought and likens it to a dead plant. A positive person who maintains a positive thought is likened to an ever-green plant. I learnt, through Dr. Leaf's research findings, that our physical bodies were not designed to harbor negative energy. Negative thoughts over time have a deleterious effect on our bodies.

THE STEADFAST MIND

Isaiah 26:3 says, "Thou wilt keep him in perfect peace, whose mind is stayed on thee: because he trusteth in thee." A steadfast mind is one that is unshakable in faith and fellowship with God. Our spirit is the very organ, the very center, for us to commune with the Lord. Romans 8:6 says that the mind, set on the Spirit, is life and peace.

The proper direction for the mind to gravitate is toward the Lord; the enemy entices our mind towards vain distractions of the world. The moment you entertain thoughts that are not of God, it means you have taken your eyes off Him and you have gone off tangent in your Christian walk. It means you have lost your way and you need to pray and ask the Lord to lead you back on the straight and narrow path. Whatever you accord your daily focus on is your god. When your mind is set on something other than the Lord, you are under idolatrous attack.

Strongholds are birthed through deception. A stronghold is a wrong or faulty thinking pattern brought about by deceptive external influence. Therefore, when the enemy robs you of your sound mind, he enslaves you into fear and disbelief; thus, rendering you ineffective and without impact. Whatever you give your attention to, will eventually influence the sensation of your heart, which in turn greatly influences your thought pattern. Keep your heart with all diligence; for out of it are the issues of life. (Proverbs 4:23). The Word of God says, "Take every thought captive" (See 2 Corinthians 10:5).

INTIMACY WITH THE LORD BREAKS STRONGHOLDS OF THE MIND

A solid relationship with the Lord is mandatory to have success in all the other areas of life. Intimacy with the Lord means having a deep, committed, personal relationship with Him. It entails consistent dialogue with the Lord; touching base with Him every moment through prayer and maintaining right thinking through meditation on God's Word. This is the key to breaking demonic strongholds over our lives. I pray with my husband at 3am every morning. I also pray in the morning with my prayer partner before I fully start the day. Having a specific time to pray promotes discipline in your relationship with the Lord. I call it having an appointment with the Holy Spirit. While it is important to have a specific time to pray, it is also important to understand that intimacy with the Lord is including Him in your day to day activities by operating according to His Word and instructions. You can talk with God while at the supermarket, while you are in the shower, while you are cleaning the house, wherever you may be.

How is your relationship with the Lord? How would you rate your intimacy level? How often do you pray? Are your eyes focused on Him or are you distracted by this counterfeit world?

THE FEAR OF THE LORD CAN SHIFT YOUR MINDSET

The Word of God says, "The fear of the Lord is the beginning of wisdom" (Proverbs 9:10). The fear of the Lord does not carry a negative connotation. Having the fear of the Lord means having a reverential awe of Him and doing whatever is required to serve Him in spirit and in truth (See John 4:24). If one does not fear God, it means you do not take sin seriously or you do not have a serious understanding of the enormous consequences of sin. Darkness and light cannot co-exist. Sin therefore separates you from God, who is your source of life:

"For the wages of sin is death, but the gift of God is eternal life through Christ Jesus our Lord." (Romans 6:23).

When I was going through my spiritual mindset shifting, I realized that I developed a greater fear of the Lord. Attending that deliverance ministry opened up my eyes to the demonic world and I had a more profound understanding of the consequences of sin. That consequence is a strong demonic oppression of the mind.

When I travelled for the first time with the intention of spending only three weeks, I realized that the Lord was not releasing me to travel back to Jamaica. I developed what I call "radical faith." Radical faith, in my definition, is crazy faith. Crazy faith means believing God against all odds, irrespective of what the physical realm illustrates. The Lord was telling me to resign from my job of over ten years. I was praying about what the Lord said: *you know, just making sure it was not the devil.* Of course, I, like most of us, said that I was praying about the instructions of the Lord for approximately one year, even though, very deep within, I knew it was Him. My flesh had certainly been dominating me and caused me to keep buying time in the name of seeking God's will. God had already spoken. He had already instructed me clearly.

After questioning the voice of the Lord for so long, there was no room for any more prayer, no more excuses. The reverential fear of the Lord came upon me so strongly at that point, that I would not have dared to continue living in disobedience. I had to repent and ask the Lord for forgiveness for acting in disobedience for so long. The Spirit of the Lord instructed me: "Remain in the United States to complete your spiritual transformation."

On the morning of that day of submission, I awoke with an ambiguous feeling. In retrospect, I wondered why I had this feeling after I was the one who sought the Lord in prayer and fasting to show me my purpose. God must have been thinking: "This child is so confused." I knew I heard from God and it was time to use my formula. *My mind was made up*, I sought the Lord through *prayer,* and He answered me; now it was time to take *faith-driven action*. I took my laptop, typed the resignation letter and prayed again. The enemy started to whisper in my ears, "You have lost your independence. How will your mortgage be paid? How will your utilities be paid?"

My finger was seconds away from clicking send when I asked, "Lord, are you sure?" I felt peace and there it went. When I resigned, I felt like a weight was lifted off my shoulders. I experienced complete peace about staying when I sent in that resignation. Was it scary? Oh, it definitely was. It was the biggest decision I ever had to make at that point in my life; it was bound to make me nervous. It certainly was not the perfect situation or condition to quit my job, but I have since learnt that when the Lord speaks, obedience is the only response.

THE FEAR OF THE LORD YIELDS RESULTS

When the Lord gives an instruction, you do not have a choice but to obey; obedience is mandatory. Disobedience will take you through a vicious cycle of false glory before failure. Fearing the Lord means having complete obedience, even though what the Lord is asking you to do makes no sense through your mortal eyes. I trusted the Lord and it yielded many results.

My spiritual transformation continued in total peace. I began to have dreams and visions and experienced the fullness of the Lord's joy like I never did before. I had many angelic visitations, many dreams and visions, and many eye-opening spiritual encounters that catapulted my faith.

Apart from my spiritual catapult, within that time, the following also took place:

1. I got married to my husband. He has been a complete blessing in my life. God will always link purpose with purpose.

2. God spoke to me concerning a deliverance manual which has formed Part Two of this book.

3. I knew the Lord called me to be of service to hurting women. Within that time, I completed the plan for my Women's Foundation.

Had I not been obedient to the voice of the Lord, I would not have had these amazing experiences.

RETURNING BACK HOME

When I returned to Jamaica, I was a different person. The person who went on the plane was certainly not the same person who came back to Jamaica. I returned home with a more elevated spiritual mindset.

I had a very long conversation with the Lord. I said, "Lord, now that You told me to resign my job and now that I am back home, what am I going to do with myself? Lord, I did Banking for most of my work life. What do I do with myself now?" I began to move in faith by flooding the market with applications. I said, "Lord, with that radical spiritual transformation, I just cannot doubt you now." Soon after, I landed a job through a friend as a Sales Manager at a Sales Management company that was into mind transformation. My success formula certainly worked again. This was the start of the second phase of my mindset transformation. When I started at this new company, it re-ignited a new career fire inside me.

CHAPTER 4
THE EFFECT OF MINDSET ON FINANCES

Poverty is a spirit. The open door for this spirit into your life is the quality of your thoughts. If you continue to think at what I call a "ground level", you will not experience the abundance of God. Ground level thinking is mediocre thinking and the harnessing of self-limiting thoughts that hold you in bondage. It is impossible to escape the bondage of poverty, if your mindset is not elevated.

As an individual, you must decide which state of mind you intend to entertain. Your financial prosperity is wrapped up in the condition of your mind and what you have accepted to be true. If you have financial challenges and you are experiencing consistent lack, it is time to take a closer look at the condition of your mind. What are you thinking about and focusing on? Certainly, whatever you tend to meditate on will indeed come to pass. If you focus on and continue to speak about lack, that will become your reality. On the flipside, if you want to become wealthy, meditate on it, study it and speak about it daily. This way, undoubtedly, wealth will become your reality. If you focus on wealth, your mind will acquire the taste of wealth. The condition of your mind will affect your financial growth.

DECIDE TO STEP OUT OF POVERTY

Everything in life can be addressed by a decision. You are a decision away from a changed life. As mentioned in Chapter One, when you become "sick and tired" of living in poverty, you will make a decision to step out of it. How can one step out of poverty? It starts with guarding the door of your mind. Many stories are told of the man who won a million dollars and became broke after a short time. This man had the money, but his mind was not renewed.

He did not have the mindset it took to manage his newly found wealth. It was like pouring new wine in an old wineskin or patching up an old garment with new fabric.

"No one sews a patch of unshrunk cloth on an old garment, for the patch will pull away from the garment, making the tear worse. Neither do people pour new wine into old wineskins. If they do, the skins will burst; the wine will run out and the wineskins will be ruined. No, they pour new wine into new wineskins, and both are preserved." (Matthew 9:16-17 - NIV).

How we live our lives is a manifestation of our state of mind. A man with a poverty mindset will continue to find himself in lack, while the man with an abundant mindset will find wealth and riches pursuing him. A man with an elevated mindset, which is one of creativity and optimism toward money, will attract positive opportunities for wealth creation.

Holding yourself 100% responsible for your financial state is the first step to improving your financial state. Therefore, when you begin to accept responsibility for your financial state or position, you have actually taken the first step towards changing it. Shifting blame to someone or something for your financial challenges will not help.

Developing the right mindset toward money will aid all areas of your life. The right mindset comes from self-examination. You really need to get to a place of honesty about your finances. Ask yourself these questions and be honest with the reply to self. They are aimed at self-examination regarding financial mindset. They determine if your mindset is right for financial authority:

1. Do I have a monthly budget?
   ANSWER: _____

2. How much of my money is spent wastefully?
   ANSWER: _____

3. Do I save? If not, why not?
   ANSWER: _____

4. How disciplined am I towards saving?
   ANSWER: _____

5. Do I spend more than what I earn?
   ANSWER: _____

6. Do I put on a facade to appear richer than I am?
   ANSWER: _____

7. Am I honest with myself about the balance in my bank account?
   ANSWER: _____

8. Am I pretending that the credit card which keeps accumulating interest monthly does not exist?
   ANSWER: _____

9. Am I not answering the phone because the bank, utility company or my friend that I borrowed money from is calling me?
   ANSWER: _____

10. Do I avoid talking to my spouse about financial matters?
ANSWER: _____

These questions are a mirror to your financial mindset. The more you become honest with yourself, the more you will step out of poverty. You cannot fix something unless you admit that it is broken. You cannot take something to a repair shop unless you acknowledge that it is broken. God wants to restore you to your rightful place of abundance, but for Him to step in, you must acknowledge that you need help. Some of us do not admit that we need help because we are afraid to appear weak. It takes a strong person to acknowledge a weakness and ask for help. If you are not strong in the area of finance, ask for help today.

When I was working at the bank, I remember one particular year when I had a huge problem with my finances. I found myself borrowing to be able to make it through the following month. This became a vicious cycle that continued for about four months. I knew I was in bondage and it produced such an unsettling feeling. At that point, I knew I was not being honest with myself about my finances. I had to make a decision to start working with a strict budget, in order to pull myself out of that financial stress hole.

YOU WILL HARVEST THE SEED SOWN

When you plant an apple seed, you should certainly expect an apple tree to spring up. If you plant a mango seed, can one expect grapes? Everything on earth operates under the seed and harvest principle: "You only reap what you sow." Every seed reproduces after its own kind. You must be prepared to reap the seed that you have sown or that which was sown by authorities above you. We plant seeds every day without even realizing it: seeds of anger, seeds of bitterness, seeds of charity, seeds of love, etc. In your day to day activities at home, work and church, do you realize that you are planting seeds every day? Even your speech is submitted to this principle; every word that comes out of your mouth will manifest after itself; you must therefore think before you speak. Matthew 12:36 says: "But I say unto you, that every idle word that men shall speak, they shall give account thereof in the day of judgment." We must be conscious of the seed that we are planting.

Understanding the Scriptural concept of reaping what you sow is quite significant. The man who works for a year and spends all he has without a clear vision or agenda, is sowing a seed of poverty. If you wear your tithe money in the form of dresses or shoes, the devourer will show up at your door (See Malachi 3:10-11). Essentially, there are consequences to each one of your thoughts, words and actions. The seed you plant today is what you will reap tomorrow.

"Be not deceived; God is not mocked: for whatsoever a man soweth, that shall he also reap." (Galatians 6:7).

This is a powerful Scripture and happens to be the one I live my life by. It is applicable in all areas of life.

MONEY MINDSET

What is your relationship with money? Do you realize that you have one? This relationship, like most other relationships, can be either healthy or toxic. Your relationship with money is dependent on how you perceive money. It is greatly influenced by how you were conditioned in your foundational years to think about money. When you were a child, did you hear statements such as the following:

1. "We can't afford this."
2. "I don't have any money."
3. "We don't need money. All we need is Jesus."

4. "We will be having a birthday party."
5. "We are going to Disney."
6. "We are buying a house/car."

What you grew up hearing affects your perception of the world. If you grew up hearing 1-3, you will most likely approach the world from a different perspective from the child hearing 4-6. It is important to understand what paradigm you are in on the topic of money.

How do you feel about money?

Are you comfortable talking about money?

Do you think having money is a bad thing?

Your money mindset is a set of beliefs that you acquired over time based on your life experiences. Your money mindset are those thoughts and feelings that drive your belief towards money. How you feel toward money will affect your ability to attract it. Since everything starts in the mind, it is important to examine your thoughts on the matter.

A person who grew up from a place of lack will believe that JA$50,000 is a lot of money. On the other hand, a person who grew up from a place of abundance may perceive JA$10,000,000 as a drop in the ocean. An abundant thinker will have no attachment to money; to such, it is merely a means of exchange. Such a person will therefore not struggle bringing themselves to tithing and doing charitable activities. The person coming from a place of lack will do the complete opposite; a poor man hoards and attracts more poverty in the process because, unless a seed falls to the ground and dies, it cannot reproduce of its own kind. From a financial perspective, hoarding means to have an intense attachment to money. It means holding on to your money so tightly that you find it difficult to tithe, help others or do any form of charitable financial activity. This creates greater lack. The Bible says: "Give, and it shall be given unto you; good measure, pressed down, and shaken together, and running over, shall men give into your bosom. For with the same measure that ye mete withal it shall be measured to you again." (Luke 6:38).

I am certainly not saying you should give away all you have. In fact, my monthly routine is to take out my tithe, then my savings, then everything else flows from there. It is of paramount significance to save. The abundant thinker will understand that there needs to be a balance. What mindset do you have towards money? Are you a hoarder or an abundant thinker?

What Are You Focusing On?

Having a steadfast focus through the habit of concentration is one of the keys to financial progress. Whatever you are focusing on will eventually manifest. Whatever you are focusing on will become your reality. Therefore, if you focus on poverty, you will be poor and that will not change. If you focus on the illness that you went to the doctor about last week, you will not get better. If you focus on wealth, then wealth will find you. Simply put, you attract to your life what you focus on. Begin to focus on the good things you want to happen in your life.

You may think, "This is easier said than done." But I dare to say, "It is not!" The same energy you take to focus on the negative, is the same energy you can use to focus on the positive. Self-awareness is key in this exercise. You have read in the earlier chapters of this book that self-awareness requires practice to master. When you become self-aware, you will recognize when a negative thought comes up in your mind. At that point, switch that negative to positive and experience its wonderful effects. If you do not become self-aware, minor things will steal your time and energy. If something pops up during the day, before you react to it, you must ask yourself these questions: "Is this major or minor? How will this affect my financial goals that I have planned for today?" We are powerful beings and we have the power to choose whatever we want to focus on.

GET OUT OF DEBT

"Owe no man anything…" (Romans 13:8a).

I love this Scripture. What a powerful reminder. Can you imagine waking up in the morning and knowing you are debt free? In fact, exercise the power of imagination right now. Take some time and imagine what it would be like to be financially free. How does it feel? At the time of writing this book, I am not there yet, but that is certainly where I am aspiring to be. Like me, you probably have a car note or a mortgage, and that is okay. The important thing is to know that you are working towards the level of financial independence where you don't owe anyone. Working toward that level of financial freedom requires an intentional deliberate effort. You must write down your plan in a step by step process, then embark on the execution of your tasks within the plan.

What is your bank account balance looking like right now? What is your credit card looking like right now? Are your expenses greater than your income right now? If they are, you are not in a good place. I challenge you to take a pen and paper right now and begin to write down who you owe. Write your clear plan towards clearing those debts within the next three to six months. Remember the power of a "made up mind" as you read earlier. If you have a large debt, you may have to structure the repayment over a longer period of time. It is important to have realistic goals. When you have a realistic plan and deliberate actions towards your goals, things will begin to happen that will lead you to their accomplishment.

If you are married, schedule a day in the week to talk about money matters with your spouse. If you are single, take a day in the week to look back through your personal budget. You can do it with a trustworthy friend or family member, if you wish. You must stop pretending that the bills do not exist. If fact, the faster you can pay off your debt, the better you are.

The truth is, most of us owe somebody something, even if it is just a small loan from a friend. Unless you were born into a wealthy family or received a huge inheritance, you will owe somebody something. What should be noted is that heavy focus should be placed on paying off that debt as soon as possible, so you can have peace of mind. If you have a big mortgage, you can start by paying the principal of that mortgage when you have extra funds. This payment should be separate from your regular monthly payments. Applying this extra money to the "principal only" will significantly reduce the "interest" on the facility. This will result in less money being paid compared to the original contractual agreement over the life of the loan.

Some will say debt is not a bad thing. You will argue that some debt is good, like taking a loan to go to school, purchasing your home or a car, etc. Those, in my opinion, are justifiable debts. The debt that one should not accrue is a loan to go shopping, take a casual trip or taking a credit card just because the bank told you that you qualify for one. Remember, the point is, whatever debt you have acquired over the years, you need to have a strategic plan to pay it/them off as soon as possible. In my opinion, if you have enough cash to make a direct purchase, avoid debt and pay cash.

Financial Independence Is Awesome

Poverty is awful; financial independence is awesome. Financial independence is having the ability to live off your personal resources. Having financial security allows you to enjoy peace of mind. Having the ability to go to a store and picking up what you want without looking at the price, will put a smile on your face. Financial independence does not come overnight; it requires planning and not just what I would call "willy nilly" planning; it requires meticulous planning. It requires making a budget and being disciplined enough to follow it. Financial independence requires the discipline of saving.

Have you thought about your life ten years from now? You certainly do not want to be at the same place you are right now. Ten years from now, I am sure you expect to be at a better place financially. You want to experience that awesome feeling of being able to afford what you want in life. To experience this, you must begin to think strategically and position yourself to receive financial independence. What do you see yourself doing ten years from now or even five years from now? Maybe travelling the world, owning your first car, buying your first or another home, owning your business, etc. Examine where you are right now; are you positioned to achieve your dream within that time frame? What are you doing today to ensure you are positioned to accomplish your dream within the timeframe you have set for yourself?

Investing in Self

When I came back to Jamaica and started my new job as a Sales Manager, my mindset toward my finances shifted as I went deeper in my research on the power of the mind. I worked in a very small office and thus worked very closely with the CEO and General Manager of the company. These two gentlemen were excellent at what they did. It was a highly energized environment. I started to do research on the lives of successful men and women. I studied what made them successful, what habits they had and what kept them motivated. I quickly started to get a deeper understanding of terms such as visualization, affirmations, verbalization, etc. The materials I read and videos I listened to were not anything new to me, but it seemed like I was hearing/reading them for the first time. There really is nothing new under the sun. Your perception really depends on the state of mind and season you are in at the time. Based on my season and my environment, I attracted a different level of thinking, particularly in the area of finance.

I started to dedicate time for self (blocking time to train my mind and my thoughts). It is very important to spend time with self as it allows you to discover things about yourself that you didn't know existed. Quiet time is of paramount significance; do not run away from it.

I soon began to listen to videos on mind transformation and read books on the power of the mind. I studied wealth and delved deeper with my study of successful men and women. Since I knew I was pre-disposed to poverty based on my family background, I worked assiduously on getting my mind to understand that becoming successful required a deliberate push. I became extremely excited through my research. I thought to myself, "Why was I not edifying myself with these materials all along?"

I bought my home at age twenty-seven and my first car at age twenty-eight. Of course, I felt like I had accomplished the world at that point. When I started edifying myself on the power of the mind and reading mind transforming materials, I started to speak differently. I remember thinking to myself, "If only I knew then what I know now." I was not beating myself up, I merely realized that I was entering a higher realm of learning and consciousness. I pause here to say that it is very important to:

- Have a good mentor.
- Surround yourself with the right people.
- Teach your children to read empowering materials at an early age, so the significance of living a purposeful life becomes ingrained in their minds from early.

When I started to understand the power of the mind, I wanted to use all this powerful information immediately. I began to place affirmation in my home at strategic places: in my bathroom, in my bedroom and in front of the couch where I would normally sit when I get home from work. I recorded "I AM" affirmations on my phone and played and repeated them as soon as I got into my car. I was now at the point where my spiritual transformation and financial mindset was elevated to another level. I coupled my research information with Biblical principles, and I found myself at a very powerful place. As a child of the highest God, I began to have a firmer belief and understanding in using my own mind and will power, coupled with the Word of God, to get what is already mine.

PRAYER AND PROCRASTINATION

I came to the realization that one of the problems in the body of Christ is that we use prayer as an excuse for not taking action. Procrastination is the art of delaying. As a child of God, I believe in the Scripture that ask us to pray without ceasing (See 1 Thessalonians 5:17). However, I believe that once you have prayed a while, and listened a while, there comes a time to move into action. Faith without works is dead (See James 2:26). The Christian procrastinator continues to seek God for clarity and provision to move, even when God has already spoken. Two, three or even ten years later, this Christian will still be seeking the Lord on a matter. The Bible has the answer to life's challenges. Whatever the situation that presents itself, ask yourself the question, "What does the Bible say about this matter?" Alongside praying, you must apply the wisdom of God.

Six months into praying about resigning from the bank, I knew the Lord had spoken to me about resigning. However, I claimed that I was praying about it. I received one confirmation after another. I had to admit to myself that I was seeking the Lord on something that He had already spoken to me about. This is plain procrastination and disobedience, wrapped up in religious acts. I had to repent about it. I agree; issues will arise in life that require diligent prayer and fasting for direction. I however do not condone laziness wrapped up in prayer. Be diligent in searching God's Word about the matter, and when He has instructed you to act, do it without hesitation. Many God-given opportunities have been missed because of this kind of procrastination.

There are times when it seems as though the Lord is so quiet on a matter of great concern to you. It almost feels like God is hiding from you. In a situation of this nature, you must examine a number of things:

1. **How well are you listening?** God talks to us, but many times we are too busy praying and wayfaring that we do not hear His voice.

2. **How is your meditation?** There are times when you need to be still before God and listen. Simply sit in quietness and meditate on His Word, as the Holy Spirit leads you.

3. **Are you asking the Lord for wisdom on the matter?** The Lord wants us to come to Him and ask Him for wisdom. If you are confused and desire wisdom on something, go to God in prayer and ask (See James 1:5). The Word of God says, "We receive not because we ask not" (See James 4:3). Check if you are praying in the flesh (your will or God's will).

You have been praying about the house, car, marriage, great job, your own business, etc. What have you actually done while you are praying? God wants us to live an abundant life. He wants you to enjoy the finer things of this life. This therefore means that God wants you to have all the things listed above. Prayer alone is not enough; you must move toward it; the operative word here is "move." You have to go to the relevant agency to put in the application for the house, go to the car mart to test drive the car prophetically, send out the job application to get the dream job, and go to the relevant body to register the business. You must leave the house to meet the husband (believe me, you will not meet him by sitting at home). You continue to speak about the things you desire but you do not "move." Get up and go towards it. Often, the excuse is that you are waiting to hear from God in order to move, yet God has already spoken. God is saying, "Go ahead and I will release angels to aid you. I will favor you." While you are waiting on God, God is waiting on you to "move" and claim what is yours.

I challenge you to grab pen and paper. Yes, go ahead and begin to write down what you are believing God for. I dare you to think big while you are at it. Ask big in order to receive big. As you engage in prayer and fasting, begin to move. Yes, get up and go towards what already belongs to you. Do not be the child of God who prays every day, asking God for what He already dispatched to you through His Word. If He said it, it is done! All you need to do is move into action according to His principles. Procrastination and indecisiveness are not of God. It is time for you to walk as a kingdom child of God.

WRONG THINKING ABOUT MONEY

When my mindset shifted in the area of finance, it became clearer to me that poverty is a choice. I can recollect when I was a child, I kept hearing in church that money was evil; just stay humble, the riches are in heaven, what you do not receive here on earth, you will receive in heaven. That is nonsense! Your abundance is here and now. Go and get it now. Nothing is wrong with money; it is the love of money that is evil (See 1 Timothy 6:10). How can you be of assistance to someone who is poor, if you are poor yourself? Will you just pray for someone who is hungry on the road without feeding him? Is your desire to have just enough wealth for yourself and your family?

"If a brother or sister be naked, and destitute of daily food, and one of you say unto them, Depart in peace, be ye warmed and filled; notwithstanding ye give them not those things which are needful to the body; what doth it profit?" (James 2:15-16).

I believe that to first minister to someone as a Christian, I must be living the life that will attract an unbeliever to the God that I serve. I must be walking wealthy for him/her to ask me about the God that I serve. Nobody wants to serve a broke, dead God. The first step to attracting wealth is to change your mindset to towards money.

MANIFESTATION: SHIFTED MINDSET

As I continued on my path to an elevated mindset, my circumstances began to change; my subconscious mind began to open up to affirmative statements. One beautiful morning, I got up and saw my small car parked in my garage. It was the first time in a long time that I took a good look at the car I was driving for over three years. Suddenly, I realized that my car needed to be changed. I realized that I was driving a small car that was nine years old.

I must pause to highlight the fact that sometimes we are living in a cage and we do not know it. In that season of my life, I started to step out of the cage into a realm of limitless possibilities. Due to my shifted mindset, and this surprising discovery, I immediately began to look at cars online. I didn't get a chance to visit a car dealership due to my busy days. Two weeks later, after viewing cars online, I received a call from a popular car company for an interview.

78

"Wow!" I thought, "I don't even remember sending out an application to this place."

As I drove in that morning to attend the interview, I smiled as I saw the car of my heart. This call came because I opened myself up to the possibility of owning a new car. The car I was looking for then began looking for me. The company had a huge sale on the brand new 2019 Suzuki Vitara (fresh on the market) with one million dollars off. This brought me back to when I was purchasing my home. Indeed, I did apply my success formula. I proceeded to pray and believe even more that I would have that car. As I began to gather the documents, by the time I went back, there was another one million dollars off. I ended up purchasing a brand-new vehicle for two million dollars less than its original value. This happened as a result of prayer, a made-up mind and taking action. The angels moved in my favor because I moved in faith. That two million dollars off allowed my monthly payments to be right where I could afford it at the time. One popular author said, "What you are looking for is looking for you."

When you begin to pray, declare, decree and affirm, everything starts to line up. Suddenly you begin to meet people; phone calls begin to come in and opportunities comes knocking at your door. Words are powerful, the Bible says ask and you shall receive (See Matthew 7:7). The same strength it takes to ask for the small, is the same strength it takes to ask big. Knock and it shall be opened. If I didn't move toward the opportunity, which came in the form of an interview, I would not have identified the car that was sitting on the car lot waiting for me. I did not get that job, but I believe the Lord orchestrated that interview for me to find the time to look at the car. Seek and you shall find.

There is a time and season for everything. When I purchased my home, it was the time and season for it. Similarly, when I purchased my car, it was the perfect time when the company had the sale. You must ask the Lord for wisdom in knowing when to take action. Time lost cannot be regained. Do not allow your opportunities to pass you by. It is the will of God for you to prosper, but He will not descend from His throne to hold your hand and drag you in the physical. Grab a pen and paper and begin to write what you want, then pray, then move. Yes, get up and go get what is yours.

THE POWER OF AFFIRMATIONS

Affirmations have such a positive effect on your mind. When I started to do daily affirmations about my wealth and prosperity, my financial state changed significantly.

Note very carefully, you must believe the affirmations you are making. Begin to make these financial declarations and watch how your subconscious mind moves into action:

1. I am a money magnet. Money comes to me from the North, South, East and West.

2. I am financially free and financially blessed.

3. I am an expert at what I do and deserve to be paid for my time, skills and knowledge.

4. I have a healthy relationship to money, and I am an abundant thinker with an elevated mind-set.

5. Every dollar I spend and donate comes back to me seven-fold.

6. I constantly attract opportunities that create more money.

7. I am competent to handle large sums of money and large projects.

8. Money expands my life opportunities and experiences.

9. I am surrounded by wealth and attract people with a kingdom mind-set.

10. I am divinely guided in investments. I believe that God accumulates and distributes His wealth through me, to be a blessing to others.

CHAPTER 5
THE EFFECT OF MIND-SET ON PHYSICAL WELL-BEING

How will you achieve success in your purpose, if you are struggling to patch up the health of your body? It is impossible to live an effective life with a damaged body. Many things affect the functioning of your body, but in this chapter, I want to focus on one of the most important factors: the state of mind.

There is a direct correlation between your mental and emotional state, and the state of your physical body. When I began to study the mind and how it works, I was amazed at how important it is to maintain positive thoughts. Positive thoughts bring radiance to your body; it makes you walk around smiling without even realizing it. Positivity brings happiness and allows you to light up a room when you enter. Negative thoughts, on the contrary, are toxic to your body. The human body was not designed to stay in a negative state. For instance, adrenaline, the hormone produced under stressful conditions, was meant to assist the human body to handle the situation at hand. Commonly known as a 'fight or flight' hormone, it causes the body to be in a heightened state of alertness and pressure, which helps a person escape or fight through a dangerous situation. Adrenaline is meant to be a defensive hormone, which is produced temporarily and in the very short term, then subsides once you are out of danger or an unpleasant situation. Prolonged exposure to adrenaline is toxic to the body, as it affects all endocrine systems, thus affecting the entire physiology of the body. Constant or frequent negative thoughts cause chronic stress, which causes prolonged exposure to adrenaline. Your body then begins to experience health issues. This explains why the thoughts you harbor in your mind manifest in your countenance.

Exercise and having a proper diet will surely have a positive effect on your body. However, after all the exercise and eating healthy, if you do not maintain a proper mindset, you will not be able to live the long and fulfilling life that you may desire. Have you ever heard stories of people who ate healthy and exercised regular, yet died suddenly and pre-maturely? This is a surprise to many as the first thing you will hear is that "but he/she was always eating so well and exercising." This is because exercise alone does not guarantee good health; it must be accompanied with a healthy state of mind. Examine the man who walks around with a sulking face; is it as a result of all the happy thoughts he has in his head? Pure, wholesome happy thoughts will result in a happy face of radiance, which in turn tends to postpone aging.

WHAT IS YOUR PRESENT STATE OF BEING?

How you think and how you feel creates your state of being. Every day we go through a routine: we wake up, take a shower, grab some coffee, drop the kids at school, drive to work, drive back home, etc. Soon your mind becomes programmed to the repetitive activities of our bodies and our bodies respond to our state of minds. It becomes a vicious cycle, which makes us become robots to our daily routine. At some point in that routine, you will develop some bad habits, for example, not eating properly because of how busy you have become. By the time you get to the place of realizing it, something drastic has happened. You then attempt to make changes, but your subconscious mind is already programmed a certain way. Attempting to do anything new or different from the robotic state makes your subconscious mind uncomfortable and, therefore, is perceived by your subconscious mind as a problem. Your mind therefore tends to resist the change and your body follows suit. It is prudent to always be conscious of your present norm and how it is affecting you. You must be conscious of how the present norm is pulling you away from who you truly are. In the business of life, you may find yourself doing things that are outside of your character and purpose, without even realizing it. If you continue to do these things over time, they become your norm. Therefore, you must do a mental recap at the end of each day. You should sit in quietness and ponder over the things that you did, as a way of staying in line with your purpose and well-being. Essentially, what you are doing here is checking in with yourself or, what I call, evaluating your present state. In fact, what I do during the day is to take a five or ten minute break whenever I feel overwhelmed to check on my present state. This is quite effective for me as it slows down the pace of my thoughts and allows me to be more conscious and alert of my state and well-being. This way, I am more productive. Doing this is especially awesome when you feel upset or anxious about something. Stopping to find out from yourself why you are feeling that way, will allow you to resolve the matter and move on with your day. Undoubtedly, this requires a high state of consciousness and self-awareness that will take a lot of practice. When I first learnt of this in a Conversation for Greatness Workshop organized by JMMB, I was amazed at the results. Believe me, this is doable.

How well are you controlling your present state? How well are you controlling your emotions in that present state?

When you get up in the morning, the first thing that comes to mind is your past experiences. More times than less, it is negative experiences that dominate your morning thoughts. These negative experiences begin to create a feeling of fear, anger and apprehension. The emotions then send messages to our brain, that ultimately reproduce self-defeating mentalities. In order to change your current state of being, there must be new thoughts that will result in healthy emotions and translate into new behavior.

Your Thoughts Can Make You Sick

Your thoughts literally drive your physical body. Getting up in the morning with negative thoughts will cause your body to adopt the feeling of the mind, which then leads to an unproductive day. Write down five things you wish to accomplish for the day and wake up with a negative mindset and see what happens. At the end of the day, you will be asking yourself, "What was I doing all day?" Having a morning filled with positive thoughts can significantly alleviate this. When you arise out of bed in the morning, the first thought you should have is one of gratefulness; being appreciative of the gift of life. Waking up with a feeling of gratefulness will position you for an awesome day.

Morning routines vary from one person to another. Let me share mine. I wake up at 3 o'clock every morning to pray and read the Word. I then read or listen to some form of inspirational/ transformational/motivational material (Dr. Myles Monroe, Les Brown, TD Jakes, Jim Rohm, etc.). I then exercise for at least thirty minutes in the house and proceed to get breakfast ready.

As I said earlier in the book, your mind speaks to your body. Therefore, you must feed your mind with strong spiritual food in the quietness of your home before you venture out into a world full of distractions. Spending quiet time in communion with the Lord is very important. This allows you to meditate on His principles and instructions, therefore, bringing things into perspective. This is very important in pulling it all together in this chaotic world. Reading inspirational materials is also feeding the mind.

In conclusion to this matter, it is important to feed your mind with transformational/motivational/inspirational food, as it feeds your physical bodies with healthy food, which is equally important. This is what will charge you up for an exceptional day. There are so many negatives out there that compete to steal your attention. Having a focused mind through a morning routine will keep the distractions at bay. If you are battling away any illness in your body, one of the first tasks on your checklist should be improving the quality of your thoughts.

CHAPTER 6
THE EFFECT OF MIND-SET ON
RELATIONSHIPS

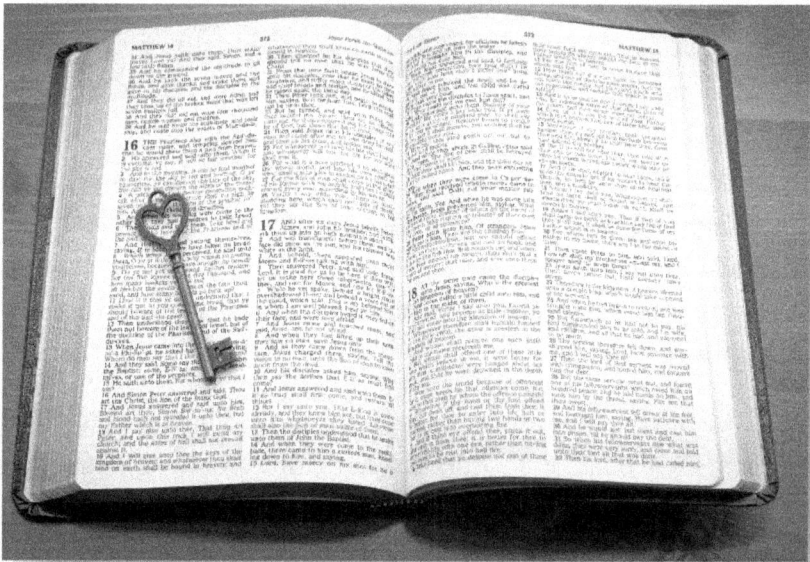

A Positive Mindset Attracts the Right People

In the first part of this book, I mentioned taking 100% responsibility for your life. In taking 100 % responsibility, you must understand that you choose the kind of people in your space. Energy attracts its kind. The people that are in your space (good/bad) are there because you attracted them according to the quality of your own mind-set.

We Attract Who We Are

Who you are is a direct manifestation of your thoughts. You act upon what you consistently think about; therefore, whatever you think about consistently is what you eventually become. 24/7, minute by minute, your mind engages you in conversation, and you must be cognizant of where you allow your mind to travel. Our minds can travel to dangerous places, if we don't guard it. There was a point in my life when I started to evaluate my contact list. As I studied it, I did not like the revelation. My personal survey proved that I was attracting more unproductive people than people worth emulating.

You attract who you are. When I gave my heart to the Lord, it represented a change in mindset and, therefore, my atmosphere shifted. I realized that there were certain calls I was not getting any more due to the shifted content of my conversations. I realized that my network circles became very small and lean due to this change in mindset. When your mindset is shifted, you begin to examine the quality of people you entertain in your space. It is not a matter of being haughty or self-centered, it is a matter of taking charge of your life. Begin to look for people who are positive and inspiring.

When I embarked on my journey of mindset transformation, my conversation changed, and I began to attract a different kind of people. Through association, I realized there are so many successful people in the world. This renewed my thinking a great deal, even in the way I handled my finances. As I followed the interaction with successful people, a fire was ignited in me for growth into a higher realm. I began to question the state of matters: "If the economy is so bad, why are they wealthy, while I am breathing in the same earth they live in? What makes them wealthy? What are they doing that I am not doing? What are the habits they have that I need to have?" When I started contemplating these questions, my mind began to expand. I started to study the lives of those successful people. Soon, success was not a foreign concept to me anymore.

BUILDING A KINGDOM MINDSET

What is a kingdom mindset? The fact that you are at this stage of reading this book means you already understand the term "Kingdom Mindset." A person with a kingdom mindset is one who understands who they are and walks in their own path of divine destiny, with boldness and authority. One with a kingdom mindset is one with an elevated mindset, who thinks in line with abundance and kingdom precepts.

You do not have to be in the physical location of a person with a kingdom mindset to tap into their mindset. You can listen to their tapes, read their books, watch them speak on the television, etc. When you are reading/listening/watching and, overall, studying these successful people, lock yourself away from all distraction. When I began to lock myself away to read and study, I would dedicate at least two hours per day to accomplish this. You must invest time and energy in order to grow your mindset into a higher realm.

The mindset you have will attract powerful people and change your life. My life is different today because of that change. My circle of friends is a lot smaller because of that shift. Understand this, it is okay to have a small circle of friends. To have one good friend with a positive mindset is better than having ten so-called friends with mediocre thinking. By shifting my mindset, I attracted a "kingdom" husband, who is a high-quality man, a powerful man of God, an Apostle and deliverance minister with two medical careers. In the process of building a kingdom mindset, you must separate yourself from the noise. Kingdom mindset attracts kingdom mindset.

THE AFTERMATH OF A SHIFTED MINDSET

Once your mindset has been shifted and you have already gone ahead and attracted people of like-mind, powerful winners with powerful mindsets, the result is phenomenal. What will happen is that you will find yourself in a circle of powerful people. You will wake up charged, exuberant and ready to win – every day! You will be fired up because the people in your space are always fired up. You will remain exuberant with a passion for excellence because the atmosphere around you is charged with the same feeling. A shifted mindset will cause you to be in the same circles with people who are supportive and want to see you living an impactful and prosperous life daily. There is one particular friend that I have, Lecia. If I ever feel down in my energy level, all I have to do is call her. Her energy is so high that each time I have a conversation with her, I become charged and ready to go again. You must have at least one person like that in your life.

A shifted mindset can have the opposite effect to what I just described. It can be a very lonely and uncomfortable place to be. You will find yourself in this space of loneliness, once you shift from mediocre to kingdom-minded. Your mediocre friends will suddenly be uncomfortable with the person you have become. Naturally, you will also have less time and energy to spare for vain chit chat and useless activity. You will want to spend every ounce of energy and every second of your day in pursuit of your divine purpose. Needless to say, you will find friends dropping off along the way.

As you build your networks with kingdom-minded people, you might find yourself at a place where nobody around your physical circles get you. You may find yourself at a place where you are still not used to your new kingdom-minded friends, yet your old friends are already uncomfortable around you. It is a lonely place to be, but do not be alarmed when it happens. Whenever you are tempted to restore your networks with your old cliques, just be patient and remember this: it is easy for you to find a bunch of negative people, than it is to find one positive person.

How Do You Find People of Like-Mind?

The first step to finding people of like-mind is to write down what you are passionate about. Go to your journal or find a piece of paper and write this heading: "THINGS THAT MAKE ME EXCITED/THINGS I AM PASSIONATE ABOUT. When you jot down those things, begin to research the places you can go to experience those things. Too many of us claim that we want to meet new people, yet we sit at home every day. I met my husband by getting myself out of my comfort zone. My friend invited me out to a political dinner meeting one Saturday evening at a hotel in Kingston, Jamaica. I was out running errands all day. I got home extremely tired, about two hours before the event. My mind began to reason: "You are tired. Just call your friend and let her know that you will not be coming." However, given that integrity is one of my core values, I had to follow through with my promise to be there. Fast forward to the event, my now husband got up to give his speech. I was sitting to the left of the room absorbing every word out of his mouth. I didn't know that I was going to meet my husband that Saturday evening. He travelled from Florida to Jamaica for that particular function and was scheduled to leave a day after the conference. If I didn't decide to get uncomfortable, I would not have met him. You must get uncomfortable to walk into purpose. Meeting people of like-mind will take a deliberate, intentional effort. You must position yourself for it. Ladies, your husband will not fall from the sky into your living room. Men, your wife will not suddenly appear when you wake from your sleep. You must go out there. Quit making excuses and make a move towards destiny.

THE DISCOMFORT OF THE MINDSET TRANSFORMATION PROCESS

Expect to feel uncomfortable when you are in the process of mindset transformation. Discomfort will come because you are being pulled out of your norm. As human beings, we are wired to process change as a problem. It is difficult for the mind to accept anything new outside of your normal routine. The norm is to have many people call you daily; the norm is to gossip and spend time with negative people. As your mindset begins to shift, you will realize that you have zero time to entertain most of the conversations you once had. You will have a zero-tolerance approach to nonsense. Your phone will ring less and there will also be a lonely feel that pops up every now and then. Take heart though, it is a part of the process. It is a part of the uncomfortable feeling that you must go through in order to grow into a higher realm. Your muscle must be broken in order to be built.

CHAPTER 7
BE STRATEGIC: PLAN AND EXECUTE!

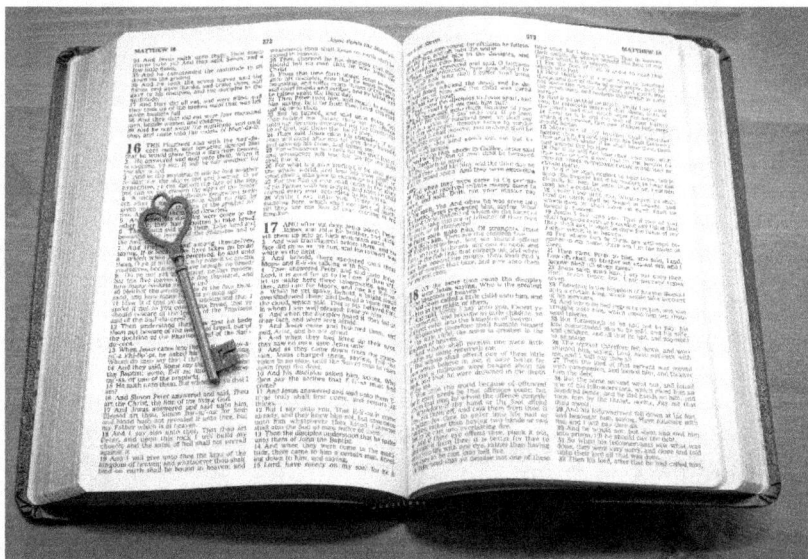

SEGMENTING YOUR LIFE

In order for purpose to manifest, it is important to segment your life. You will not be able to live a wholesome life, unless you pay attention to all aspects of your life. Examine the life of the man who is financially successful without his health or the man who is a Pastor but does not go home to his wife and children or the man who has a beautiful family but he has not positioned himself well financially. May I suggest to you that it is of paramount importance that you balance your life in these four aspects:

1. Spiritual
2. Financial
3. Physical
4. Social/relationship

Use the next few pages, with the headings already outlined, to write down your goals under each aspect, and your method of execution for each goal. Keep this book close so you can do a daily review of them. When you break down your life in these areas, it gives you a clearer and a more definitive view of how you are progressing in the different areas of your life.

When you set a goal, you must make a deliberate and intentional effort to accomplish that goal. Essentially, you must be strategic in the execution of your goals. You must do daily reviews of your goal. Having a vision board is an excellent idea because whatever you can visualize has a tremendous effect on the mind. Setting goals is one thing, but execution is quite another. You must describe in a step by step process your method of accomplishing your goals, and also apply timelines in getting them done. This will force you into action to meet the set deadlines. Please take some time, before moving into section two of this book, to write down your strategic plans for each area of your life, and how you will execute. I am a living testimony that it works. Have fun doing it.

STRATEGIC PLAN: SPIRITUAL

Goals (The What)

Execution (The How) (also outline your timelines)

STRATEGIC PLAN: FINANCIAL

Goals (The What)

Execution (The How) (also outline your timelines)

STRATEGIC PLAN: PHYSICAL

Goals (The What)

Execution (The How) (also outline your timelines)

STRATEGIC PLAN: SOCIAL/RELATIONSHIP

Goals (The What)

Execution (The How) (also outline your timelines)

BE A PROFESSIONAL GOAL ACHIEVER

Pursue your purpose professionally. Know who you are, what you want and pursue it with poise. Being a professional goal achiever means you are conscious of what your purpose is and what your goals towards it are. You have written them down on paper and are working to execute them. The professional goal achiever is self-disciplined and does not need external factors to motivate them to execute their goals. This kind of achiever is intrinsically motivated. He/she studies his/her goals and rehearses their execution mentally every day, until they become tangible reality.

You must hunger for the tangible manifestation of your goals in order to be motivated to push aggressively to their accomplishment. Don't be mindful of what others have to say about you. Put on your focus glasses and do not look to the left, neither to the right. Knowing who you are and what you are about is of crucial importance. This is essential because there will always be someone ready to distract you with their skewed opinion of who you are, who you are not and who you should be. People can be very opinionated when it comes to your life. If you don't know who you are, you will be driven off your course by others' opinion of you. This is what you should do: wake up in the morning and tell yourself who you are, what you are about, and what you will accomplish for that day. My suggestion to you is that you work your day job diligently, but while you are working your day job, exercise your mind every second of the day on how you can build your own destiny and legacy. Be thou greedy in building your own dream. Am I saying quit your job and build you dream? Absolutely not! I am saying give your day job 110% and use that capacity to discover what you

104

do well, then turn that into a money-generating dream. You will find yourself doing what you love and making money while doing it. Go forth and professionally accomplish your goals and push toward your dream.

REMAIN OPTIMISTIC

The eyes of the pessimist and the optimist both view the same glass filled halfway with water. However, the mind of the pessimist perceives the glass as half empty, while the mind of the optimist perceives the glass as half full. It is important to remain optimistic in your life's journey. Having a positive thought in the morning will affect your entire day. Having a positive attitude throughout life will produce progress in all areas of your life. Do not become dismayed if you are not progressing according to your timelines: slow progress is still progress. Go back to the drawing board and start again, if the situation calls for it. The most successful people you meet will tell you about the many failures they had in life, before they got to the place they are right now.

CREATE SUCCESS FOR YOURSELF: DO NOT DEPEND OR WAIT ON THE SUCCESS OF OTHERS

Do not depend on the success of others to progress in your own life. Do not remain in the shadow of anyone. You were born a leader in your own right. God has given you giftings and talents, go bold with them. If you are a Mechanic, be the best mechanic ever. If you are a Teacher, be a leader in the teaching industry. Just go bold with your gift and talent; do not hold yourself back for anything.

Do not wait on the success of others. It may never happen. While you are sitting and waiting, you could have been creating success for yourself. Creating success for yourself means going after your own purpose and staying in your lane, while you push ahead. Creating your own success also means building your own legacy. You cannot depend on your mother, father, husband or wife to bring you success. There are many things out there with your name on it and every day that passes by without you being diligent in going after what is yours, is a day wasted which will never be recovered. If you are waiting on benefitting from the success of others, it may never happen, but if you are working diligently towards yours, you are sure to see it come to pass sooner or later.

God has created us all for something great. We are all called to do something different in this world. No matter how small it is, do it to the best of your ability and leave your mark. Someone is waiting for you to step into your purpose; someone's life depends on it. There is a group of people out there who will never walk into their purpose until they hear your voice; they will never walk into their purpose until you get out there and start walking in yours. You are obligated to carry out that which God has called you to do and to be. This fact is not up for debate.

SELF-DISCIPLINE

Self-discipline is one of the key tenets of success. You must be careful of what becomes your norm. What you do day in and out will eventually become your norm. It is said that whatever you do for twenty-one days consecutively, forms a habit. Take some time now and look at what you do from Sunday to Saturday. Is whatever you are doing positive or negative? Does it promote self-development? Does it push you toward your purpose or does it promote laziness? If you realize that your assessment is leaning more towards the negative, then it is time for a change.

Begin to write down the changes you want to make. The next step is to remain disciplined in those steps. Our mind tends to focus more on the negatives than the positives. Therefore, because our focus over time becomes our reality, we tend to develop self-discipline towards bad habits and negativity, rather than towards the positive. The question is, which direction has your self-discipline taken in the four aspects of life mentioned above?

LITERATURE READINGS THAT SHIFTED MY MINDSET

Mindset transformation will not come overnight. If you want a different life, you must go in search of it. When I became dissatisfied with my life, I went in search of a different life. Essentially, I became "sick and tired", as you read earlier. The first thing I did in this search is to look at the lives of people who defied the odds and pushed their way to success. When you look at the life of a successful person, there must be some positive things that the person is doing that you can adopt. This is said within context, of course, I am not ignorant of the fact that there are people who become successful through dubious means. These are not the kind of people I am referring to here. In fact, I urge you to be very careful who you align yourself with, whether by person or through a person's literary work. Ask the Lord to give you the spirit of discernment and wisdom in knowing who to emulate. You should also develop the ability to know what to pull from a person's life or literary work and what to leave.

Studying the habits of a successful person will do you good. You do not have to re-invent the wheel; you can learn from their actions and their mistakes, their success and failures on their way there. Such role models give you a head-start. You will not have to go through what they went through to learn what they know. Only a fool learns through experience what they could have learnt from someone else's experience.

As I studied successful people, I observed that all of them live their lives a certain way. Many elements of how they perceive and go through life are common. The onus is on you to know what to pick out and adopt, and what to reject. As I said earlier in this book, when I started to study the lives of successful people, my thought-life began to shift. I started to think differently. I became more observant and meditated a lot more. This was mandatory as I had to let all that I was learning soak in. I felt like I was a sponge, just soaking everything in.

It would be remiss of me not to mention some of the materials that shifted my thinking and, subsequently, made great impact in my life. I took many lessons from these books that greatly elevated my level of thinking, as I studied through repetition.

Through continuous reading, research and studying, I came upon some statements that contributed to my shifted mindset:

1. An order that is properly given to the subconscious section of the mind will be carried out, unless it is side-tracked or countermanded by another or stronger order. ~ Law of Success by Napoleon Hill.

2. The subconscious mind does not question the source from which it receives orders, nor the soundness of those orders, but it will proceed to direct the muscular system of the body to carry out any order it receives. ~ Law of Success by Napoleon Hill.

3. Every movement of the human body is controlled by either the conscious or the sub-conscious section of the mind; that not a muscle can be moved until an order has been sent out by one or the other of these sections of the mind, for the movement. ~ Law of Success by Napoleon Hill.

4. Any idea or thought that is held in the mind, through repetition, has a tendency to direct the physical body to transform such thought or idea into its material equivalent. ~ Law of Success by Napoleon Hill.

5. There is a working relationship between the imagination, the conscious mind and the sub-conscious section of the mind. We can see that the very first step in the achievement of any desire is to create a definite picture of that which is desired. ~ Law of Success by Napoleon Hill.

6. Thoughts magnetize your entire personality and attracts to you the outward, physical things that harmonize with the nature of your thoughts. ~ Law of Success by Napoleon Hill.

7. Conduct yourself in the exact manner in which you would if you were already in possession of the object of your definite

purpose, from the moment you suggest it to your sub-conscious mind. ~ Law of Success by Napoleon Hill.

8. Every man is where he is because of the law of his being: the thoughts which he has built into his character have brought him there. ~ As A Man Thinketh by James Allen.

The greatest book that was ever written is the **Holy Bible.** It requires daily reading as it represents the key guide for your life. This book should take precedence over all other books that you read. Contained therein are the answers to all of life's issues or challenges; there is absolutely no issue in your life, which the Bible does not address. Reading the Word of God is the first step to an elevated mindset.

POWER AFFIRMATIONS THAT I USE IN THE MORNINGS:

1. I am walking in victory in all areas of my life (spiritually, financially, physically and relationship wise).
2. I plan, pray and move into action.
3. I accurately discern the voice of the Lord every day.
4. I am always calm, happy, understanding and loving.
5. I am a master at capturing all opportunities that come my way.
6. I act with love and courage always.
7. I am bold and confident all the time.
8. I am passionate, persistent and decisive.
9. Doors open for me everywhere I go.
10. I take 100% responsibility for my life: no blame or victim game.
11. I am clear on my purpose in life and disciplined to accomplish my purpose.
12. I manage my time well, and I am connected to kingdom-minded people.

PART TWO

SPIRITUAL ALERTNESS

Your mind must be lifted to a higher level of consciousness and your spiritual eyes must be opened, in order to be successful in all areas of your life. Being spiritually alert means being sensitive to what happens in the spirit. As I wrote this book and studied the Word of God, it became so evident to me that spiritual alertness is of paramount importance to abundant living. 1 Peter 5:8 admonishes us to be watchful and vigilant. If you understand that you have an enemy who monitors you 24/7, you will understand the need to remain alert. Too many people are going through suffering in different areas of their lives as a result of a lack of knowledge and consciousness. A spiritually alert person will know when the enemy is messing around with them and is causing them to behave out of character. A self-aware, sober-minded person will know when there is an open door in their life and take the necessary steps to correct the out of character behavior through repentance.

"He that covereth his sins shall not prosper: but whoso confesseth and forsaketh them shall have mercy." (Proverbs 28:13).

To be spiritually alert means to be conscious daily of where you are in the Lord. A spiritually alert person will know when they are deviating from God-given principles, while they walk on their Christian journey. The spiritually alert person is not afraid to admit when they have gone off on a tangent. They take the necessary steps to pull themselves back in line quickly. They will know when there is a demonic spirit at work in their life.

SCENARIO ON SPIRITUAL ALERTNESS

Let us consider this scenario with John. John is a devoted Christian walking the straight and narrow path. He understands the importance of having an active prayer life, so he prays every morning before leaving home. He has a family situation and is worried about the outcome. Due to the family challenge, John became very distracted in his thoughts; his energy became low and he has no more desire to pray every morning. John has become so consumed with his family situation that two months have passed without him thinking of prayer. John begins his rationalization and justification process and the enemy is gratified by the state John is in, a state of prayerlessness.

This can happen to any one of us. I can think of many distracting situations that came up, which took over my attention so much that I took my eyes off God. In this life, you must understand that unexpected things will happen every day. However, you must be able to discern when the enemy is creating a distraction to pull you off your straight and narrow. It is important to be alert to the devices of the enemy, lest he takes advantage of you (See 2 Corinthians 2:11).

God's Word does not lie (See Numbers 23:19) and cannot return to Him void (See Isaiah 55:11). His Word says, "Pray without ceasing" (1 Thessalonians 5:17). His Word says that in times of trouble or hardship, we should pray (See James 5:13). In fact, these Scriptures should not be taken lightly. They are meant for our own good. A prayerless man is a defeated man. The enemy does not want us to pray because there is power in prayer. Did you know that prayerlessness is an open door for the enemy to afflict your life?

Did you know that prayerlessness will lead you to sin? When a Christian does not pray, the flesh becomes more dominant. This is because prayer keeps your spirit man strong and keeps you in the presence of God. It is a given that the enemy does not want you to pray. Think about it, how often do you really sit before the Lord and wait on Him?

THE PRACTICALITY OF SPIRITUAL ALERTNESS

In the scenario above, John's prayer routine was disturbed by the circumstances around him. This means that weeks passed, and John did not pray; justification and rationalization stepped in. This is when the mind begins to give us a "rational" reason for doing or not doing something. This reason often makes so much sense that it makes you feel better. In this case, John begins to tell himself that he is going through a lot, his family is going through a lot and he is sure God understands why he did not have the energy to pray. In John's situation, and in all circumstances that pop up in life, we must pray without ceasing. Never stop praying.

Spiritual alertness means being conscious of when you are falling off your journey with the Lord and taking the necessary steps to get back in line. If a spiritually alert person does not pray for one or two nights, their conscience becomes greatly troubled and they start to feel as though they are losing their intimacy with the Lord. They will know when they are losing that intimacy with the Lord. They will know when they are losing their drive and desire for prayer through some kind of lethargic spirit that has sneaked up on them. The alert person will then quickly pull themselves into position. They will pull themselves from a creeping state to a standing state, then they will become restored to the powerhouse that they are in the spirit. It will not take two or three months for a spiritually alert person to notice that they are losing their desire for communion with God.

Many will say that it is easier said than done; that it just does not sound practical, with all the battles and the stresses of life. Many will say that John's case is typical of any human being and is generally acceptable given the circumstances. Is it really possible to always be spiritually alert?

Let us step out of being in a spiritually alert state a little bit. Let us consider the state of just plain alertness in all areas of life. A simple definition of being alert is a state of awareness of what is going on within one's surrounding. When you apply the matter of being sound to your physical life, how does this work? Let us consider the following questions:

1. Do you attempt to eat right?
2. Do you try to exercise at least three times per week?
3. Do you attempt to get adequate sleep?

Why do you do these things? The answer is that you want to remain physically healthy so you can live longer. I am sure you try to remain sound in these things, so you don't die before your time. Attempting to eat right, exercising and getting rest is you being alert to some of the pre-requisites of living longer. Consider the man who gets up and eats burgers, meat, drinks sodas and eat sweets every day; such a person will undoubtedly be plagued by various forms of illness and is, therefore, digging an early grave for himself. One will remain alert to the possibility of their lifespan being shortened by their unhealthy lifestyle, so they will make attempts to correct it. That is physical/health alertness.

On the matter of social relationships, there is an effort that is made to surround yourself with positive and productive people. You remain alert to the significance of doing this because you understand that the people you surround yourself with will inevitably influence your life. It is the same thing when it comes on to your family. You will remain alert when it comes to your children. You constantly monitor their behavior so you can readily recognize when peer pressure is stepping in. Is my child drinking, having sex before time, taking drugs, etc.? You exercise every possible effort to pay attention to how they are growing up.

Similarly, you remain alert to your intimate relationship to quickly pick up any change in behavior. For instance, your husband comes home by a certain time. Now he is getting home at least three hours later. You begin wondering, "Is he seeing another woman?" Your wife is no longer attentive; she is constantly on her phone, while she is at home. It leaves you wondering, "Is she cheating on me?" You quickly note the changes in your spouse's behaviour. This is an example of remaining alert in your relationship.

The same way you remain alert in the different areas of your life, is the same way you should remain vigilant in the Spirit.

Spiritual awareness is possible; it simply requires you to be conscious of who you are in Christ. Anything that challenges this knowledge, therefore, will cause immediate discomfort in your spirit, which will cause you to examine yourself and your situation in God's light. 1 Peter 5:8b says, "...the enemy goes around like a roaring lion seeking those he may devour." This means that he is in a constant state of vigilance, waiting for us to fall or weaken spiritually, in order to have an open door for him to enter our lives. If the enemy is always alert, waiting for us to miss the mark, then, why can't we be equally alert or even more? You must be alert so you can know when a door, such as prayerlessness or envy, is opening in your life for the enemy to attack you. Stay alert in order to know when you start to develop envy in your heart against your co-worker or when you feel bitter about what your mother said fifteen years ago or when you bear unforgiveness for what your husband or wife did five years ago.

The spiritually alert person will know when the spirit of lust is rising up in their heart, for example, when you are tempted to go watch porn, when you are tempted to cheat on your wife or husband with your neighbor, when you are tempted to masturbate, etc.? The spiritually alert person will notice these things rising up on the inner man and jump up from a sitting position to a standing position, putting your foot down like the powerhouse that you are in the realm of the spirit and say to yourself, "But wait"; lust is there, anger is there, bitterness is there, rejection is there, prayerlessness is there. You will be conscious and honest with yourself enough to say, "I have some things that I need to work on." You will pull yourself aside to deal with them. There is nothing wrong with locking yourself in a room and holding yourself accountable to deal with all those spirits. In fact, this is a sign of strength and maturity.

It is very important to note that when you have a personal challenge, which you are not able to handle by yourself, you must seek help. If you perceive that whatever you are facing is too difficult for you to handle, seek help from someone you can trust, not someone who will judge you, but someone who has the God-given capability and capacity to help you. The spiritually alert person will put an end to it quickly, before it festers into something uncontrollable. You have an obligation to yourself to be spiritually alert.

DEMONIC FORCES AFFECTING EVERYDAY LIFE

Demonic forces can affect one's life through many open doors, including wrong thinking. Wrong thinking is entertaining negative thoughts, ideas and intentions that lead to wrong action. The wrong action then creates an open door for the enemy to afflict your life. An open door, in this context, means an act or thought that gives the enemy legal rights or access to your life. This can be likened to hearing a gunman knocking on your door and you open the door to let him in. Essentially, this is synonymous to shaking hands with the devil. In whatever you think of or whatever you do, you are either serving the kingdom of God or the kingdom of darkness. There is no middle ground.

When you entertain negative thoughts, there is no positive action that will come out of it. Negative thoughts breathe anger, bitterness, resentment, etc. These are all demonic spirits that can enter just by you opening yourself up to a negative thought. Just to be clear, a demonic spirit can affect your life through other means such as through ancestral curse, etc.

The enemy is relentless in his pursuit of our purpose. If you do not remain self-aware, these spirits will affect your life without you knowing it.

I have listed some demonic spirits that can affect one's day to day life and activities:

- Incubus/Succubus spirit
- Compromising spirit
- Spirit of fear
- Spirit of unforgiveness
- Spirit of bitterness
- Spirit of anger
- Spirit of poverty
- Spirit of lethargy
- Spirit of perversion
- Rejection spirit
- Lying spirit
- Octopus spirit
- Spirit of oppression
- Kundalini spirit
- Python spirit
- Jezebel spirit
- Ahab spirit
- Leviathan spirit/spirit of pride
- Spirit of jealousy
- Spirit of heaviness
- Spirit of whoredom
- Deaf and dumb spirit
- Spirit of bondage
- Seducing spirits

Asmodius/Omodius/Succubus/Incubus/Night Demons/Sex Demons/Spirit Husband/Spirit Wife

Succubus/Spirit Wife

A spirit or devil in female form, that appears in dreams and takes the form of a woman in order to seduce men to engage in sexual intercourse.

Incubus/Spirit Husband

A demon in male form that lies upon a sleeping woman in order to engage in sexual intercourse with her. The incubus is usually very jealous and will not tolerate sharing his human wife or victim with anyone else. Some door openers are masturbation, pornography, fornication, lust, adultery, soul ties, pervasion, sexual abuse through molestation, rape or incest, witchcraft, indecent dressing and buying certain types of jewelry dedicated to spirits.

The objective of this demon is to impregnate the individual spiritually and emotionally. The demon plants their seed in the man or woman's subconscious to multiply unnoticed. They impregnate the individual with seeds of perversion and lust; the end result being negative emotions, feelings of condemnation and worthlessness. They want to control and subdue the individual, steal their virtue and cause nightmares to impregnate you with fear. Ultimately, the main objective of this spirit is to separate the individual from God and impregnate him/her in four ways:

1. Fear
2. Lust

3. Other spirits of sexual perversion
4. Rebellion

Incubus or succubus spirits cannot affect a person's body, unless there is an open door of disobedience, rebellion or lust that gives the spirit access or authority to physically assault him/her in that way. The open door can also be through something he or she is failing to do, that would suppress or subdue the body's natural sin nature, for example, not reading the Word enough or not praying enough. There can also be some form of compromise in the individuals own life concerning the principles of God's Word or through their association with people engaged in sin.

OPEN DOORS

- Fornication
- Masturbation
- Pornography
- Unforgiveness (cuts you off from God's grace and His protection).
- Bitterness (attracts every demon from hell to afflict your temple and life).
- Carnality (any activity that does not purposefully or deliberately build and edifies your spirit man in the things of God is a carnal activity).
- Fear and doubt (they thrive on fear to pervert your faith and strip you of your purpose).
- Witchcraft (Rebellion is open disobedience and is likened to witchcraft).

- Sexual abuse (attracts a spirit of perversion and is a doorway for fear).
- Verbal, physical and emotional abuse (they take advantage of weaknesses thus healing is necessary in all wounded areas).
- Soul-ties (being willfully, intellectually or desirably connected to a person place or thing). When your soul is tied, there is easy demonic transfer to the person, place or thing you are tied to.
- Spiritual Warfare (they take advantage of your weakness, thus if your spirit man is not fully strong, they can take advantage of your spiritual weakness while you sleep. It is important to take care of your physical body so your spiritual life can be strong).

Manifestations

- Temporary paralysis when the incubus is trying to have his way through sex in the dream realm.
- The woman experiences a strange sexual urge or wetness. She wakes up feeling like someone has made love to her or she feels someone's weight on her or between her thighs.
- The woman experiences difficulty in getting married as the spirit chases away all suitors by killing them.
- Childlessness through barrenness and miscarriages in marriage.
- Keep people single, breaks up marriages. Deceives pastors to get a divorce claiming that they will now have more time for full time ministry.

- Causes rage and anger to break relationship, causing physical abuse, emotional involvement, unnecessary jealousy.
- Will allow out of marriage relationships.
- Mastermind of matrimonial discord by creating lack of communication, betrayal, strife, cheating.
- Feeling deeply disturbed once you are awake and makes you feel emotionally and spiritually drained because they steal virtue from you.
- Frequently monitors the human wife/victim and will readily and violently attack the business, finances and health of any man who decides to marry the woman in question.

Sometimes she sees the incubus attempting to molest her, but because of the strange temporary paralysis being experienced, she is not able to break free, escape or call for help as her voice is temporarily taken.

Compromising Spirit

This is a spirit that causes you to deviate from your God-given principles and results in you being accepting of behaviors that are not Christ-like. It represents a deviation from one's principles. This compromising spirit has allowed pastors and church leaders to lose sight of their first charge. The enemy has managed to dangle "the world" before their eyes and they have opened their arms to it. This open door has led to a cloud being drawn over their eyes.

An article written by Faithlife sermons in 2019, describes the following as the manifestations of the compromising spirit:

Manifestations

- Choosing disobedience rather than obedience.
- Choosing the flesh over the Spirit.
- Choosing traditions of men over the commandments of God.
- Choosing to please others rather than to please God.
- Choosing love for this world over the love of God.
- Choosing fear of man over the fear of God.
- Choosing our own way over God's way.
- Choosing weakness over discipline.
- Choosing convenience over commitment.
- Choosing excuses over accountability.
- Choosing rebellion over repentance.

Revelation 2:20-23 - "Notwithstanding I have a few things against you, because thou sufferest that woman Jezebel, which calleth herself a prophetess, to teach and seduce my servants to commit fornication and eat things sacrificed to idols. And I gave her time to repent of her fornication, and she did not repent. Behold I will cast her into a bed, and those who commit adultery with her into great tribulation, unless they repent of their deeds. And I will kill her children with death, and all the churches shall know that I am He who searches reins and hearts. And I will give unto every one of you according to your works."

SPIRIT OF FEAR

The spirit of fear is a tormenting spirit. Fear opens the door to the devil and is connected to the lack of power and knowing who you are in Christ. The spirit of fear cannot be dealt with on a physical or natural level, it must be dealt with supernaturally. The spirit of fear is a dominating spirit that cripples the individual and ultimately results in a feeling of suppression.

Manifestations

- Being panicky
- Being nervous
- Feeling hopeless
- Hesitation
- Loneliness
- Full of paranoia and phobia
- Sleepless nights
- Insecurity
- Impatience
- Confusion
- Thoughts filled with worry
- Being uneasy and unsure
- Despair and depression
- Extreme stress
- Full of apprehension
- When your thoughts forecast doom and gloom
- Restlessness
- Being frightful
- Being anxious

Scriptures to Counter Fear

Psalm 34:4 - I sought the Lord, and he heard me, and delivered me from all my fears.

Isaiah 41:13 - For I the Lord thy God will hold thy right hand, saying unto thee, Fear not; I will help thee.

Psalm 56:3-4 - What time I am afraid, I will trust in thee. In God I will praise his word, in God I have put my trust; I will not fear what flesh can do unto me.

Deuteronomy 31:8 - And the Lord, he it is that doth go before thee; he will be with thee, he will not fail thee, neither forsake thee: fear not, neither be dismayed.

Psalm 27:1 - The Lord is my light and my salvation; whom shall I fear? the Lord is the strength of my life; of whom shall I be afraid?

SPIRIT OF UNFORGIVENESS

Unforgiveness is a grudge against someone who has offended you. It represents an open door for the enemy to torment your life (See 2 Corinthians 2:5-11). Someone who harbors unforgiveness can be likened to shaking hands with the enemy and giving him permission to come into their life. If one is struggling with unforgiveness, it becomes a major blocker to deliverance. You see, one who does not forgive, cannot be forgiven. Therefore, they clench at their own sin with their fist. This separates them from God and keeps them vulnerable to demonic attacks. The Bible charges us to be gentle with one another and forgive each other. In order to receive forgiveness, we ourselves must forgive. We have been given much in the way of forgiveness, and much is expected from us in response.

Manifestations

- You are experiencing burst of anger.
- You have a hardened heart toward the person.
- You are petty and impulsive.
- You keep a list of offences.
- You verbally and physically abuse the person.
- You desire to write off the person.
- You replay the scene over and over in your mind.
- You become sick (anxiety, depression, high blood pressure).
- You do not want to talk to the person or have them in your presence.

Scriptures to Counter Unforgiveness

Ephesians 4:32 - And be ye kind one to another, tenderhearted, forgiving one another, even as God for Christ's sake hath forgiven you.

Matthew 18:21-22 – Then came Peter to him, and said, Lord, how oft shall my brother sin against me, and I forgive him? till seven times? Jesus saith unto him, I say not unto thee, Until seven times: but, Until seventy times seven.

Luke 23:33-34 - And when they were come to the place, which is called Calvary, there they crucified him, and the malefactors, one on the right hand, and the other on the left. Then said Jesus, Father, forgive them; for they know not what they do. And they parted his raiment, and cast lots.

Matthew 6:12-15 - And forgive us our debts, as we forgive our debtors. And lead us not into temptation, but deliver us from evil: For thine is the kingdom, and the power, and the glory, for ever. Amen. For if ye forgive men their trespasses, your heavenly Father will also forgive you: but if ye forgive not men their trespasses, neither will your Father forgive your trespasses.

THE SPIRIT OF BITTERNESS

Bitterness is a spirit that will kill you slowly. It is a creeping spirit that slowly sneaks upon you, takes up residence in your heart and ultimately blows out the candle of joy and the peace of God within your soul. It is a sleeper sin that can consume you, if you are not operating at a high level of self-awareness and spiritual alertness. The root of bitterness come from one main source: injustice:

1. The feeling of not getting what you deserve.
2. When something happens to you in life that you consider to not be right.
3. When something is done to you by someone you consider to be unfair.

Manifestations

- Seeing things through an eye of pain; not being able to be objective about the situation.
- Physical ailment.
- A look of anger on the face.

- Constantly blaming the sin of the abuser, molester, adulterer as the reason for the way you are feeling.
- Sudden burst of anger and snapping.
- Not being caring, loving or gentle.
- Hypersensitivity
- Ungrateful
- Insincere
- Holds grudges
- Has mood swings

Scriptures to Counter Bitterness

Isaiah 38:17 - Behold, for peace I had great bitterness: but thou hast in love to my soul delivered it from the pit of corruption: for thou hast cast all my sins behind thy back.

Ephesians 4:31 - Let all bitterness, and wrath, and anger, and clamour, and evil speaking, be put away from you, with all malice.

Hebrews 12:14-15 - Follow peace with all men, and holiness, without which no man shall see the Lord: looking diligently lest any man fail of the grace of God; lest any root of bitterness springing up trouble you, and thereby many be defiled.

SPIRIT OF ANGER

The spirit of anger is a dark spirit that results in violence and violent like behavior. A Seminar Workbook published by the Institute in Basic Life Principles describes the following manifestations of the spirit of anger:

Manifestations

- **Irritability:** A buildup of inward tension causes an angry person to become irritated with situations and circumstances that would otherwise not bother him/her.

- **Impatience:** Unresolved anger reduces tolerance for the weaknesses and limitations of others. An angry person will often demand an instant response to his/her instructions. He/she is upset when his/her instructions are not understood.

- **Raised Voice:** Unresolved anger accompanied by impatience will often be expressed in loudness of voice. The tone will communicate harshness and lack of love.

- **Glaring Eyes:** An angry look is characterized by penetrating eyes, a pronounced frown, furrowed brows, tense facial muscles, flushed complexion, prominent veins, and enlarged pupils.

- **Hurtful Words:** A parent may wrongly express unresolved anger to a child by using harsh, unkind words and statements such as: "You are good for nothing" or "You idiot" or "I wish you were never born" or "Why can't you be like others?"

- **Explosive Actions:** Using extra force to put down an object, slamming doors or throwing things are clear evidences of unresolved anger. An angry person will usually close his/her spirit toward the one who offended or hurt him/her—as evidenced by silence, poor eye contact or avoidance.

- **Attitude of Superiority:** Wounded pride will motivate an angry person to challenge the opinions, ideas or instructions of those around him/her, especially of those in authority over him/her.

- **Increased Heart Rate:** Unresolved anger causes a more rapid heartbeat, which, in turn, requires more oxygen and causes heavy breathing. It triggers production of adrenaline in the body, which causes the heart to pump faster. This enlarges the veins, which often stand out in the neck.
- **Relational Breakdown:** An angry person will usually close his/her heart to those who offend or hurt him/her. This rejection is demonstrated by silence, poor eye contact, or avoidance; therefore, isolating the individual.

Scriptures to Counter Anger

Proverbs 14:29 - He that is slow to wrath is of great understanding: but he that is hasty of spirit exalteth folly.

James 1:19-20 - Wherefore, my beloved brethren, let every man be swift to hear, slow to speak, slow to wrath: for the wrath of man worketh not the righteousness of God.

1 Thessalonians 5:9 - For God hath not appointed us to wrath, but to obtain salvation by our Lord Jesus Christ.

Ecclesiastes 7:9 - Be not hasty in thy spirit to be angry: for anger resteth in the bosom of fools.

Psalms 37:8 - Cease from anger, and forsake wrath: fret not thyself in any wise to do evil.

THE SPIRIT OF POVERTY

The spirit of poverty attacks the mind, emotions and attitude; it is deeper than just lacking money. As mentioned in part one of this book, you cannot pray for success without taking the action toward your goals. A lazy man will fall into poverty. Proverbs 24:33-34 says: *Yet a little sleep, a little slumber, a little folding of the hands to sleep: so shall thy poverty come as one that travelleth; and thy want as an armed man.*

Through attacking the mindset, the demonic spirit of poverty will eventually attract shortages, scarcity, loss, hardship, lack, etc. Once you have attracted a poverty spirit to your life, you cannot live to your full potential and become financially free.

Manifestations

- You feel less qualified than others.
- You feel like you are in the back row of life.
- You live in the past and you constantly remember your past failures.
- You feel unambitious and think it makes no sense to pursue your goals since they feel impossible and unattainable.
- You feel fearful when it comes to pursuing your goals.
- You feel lost and procrastinate in getting things done.
- Denial: comforting oneself with words like "others are facing the same thing; everyone has debt; I am doing my best."

- You are convinced that money matters are shameful to talk about, especially in church; you feel like lack is a virtue or some kind of righteousness.
- You judge successful people as "money grabbers" or "thieves."
- You judge others and think they are shallow if they think of, learn about or act on financial matters.
- You feel you are more spiritual or mature than those who want to succeed financially. Therefore, you feel a sense of moral superiority by having less.

Scriptures to Counter Poverty

Proverbs 14:23 - In all labour there is profit: but the talk of the lips tendeth only to penury.

Psalm 34:9-10 - O fear the Lord, ye his saints: for there is no want to them that fear him. The young lions do lack, and suffer hunger: but they that seek the Lord shall not want any good thing.

Proverbs 21:5 - The thoughts of the diligent tend only to plenteousness; but of every one that is hasty only to want.

THE SPIRIT OF LETHARGY

Lethargy is a demonic spirit of fatigue or feeling sluggish.

Manifestations

- Tiredness
- Weariness

- You are exhausted all the time
- Lack of energy
- Stress and insomnia
- Decreased motivation
- Apathy
- Depression
- Infirmity
- Boredom
- Overexertion
- Allergies
- You lack spiritual passion
- You question your faith
- Chronic pain
- Eating disorders, grief, sleeping disorders, thyroid problems

Scriptures to Counter Lethargy

Isaiah 40:29 - He giveth power to the faint; and to them that have no might he increaseth strength.

Romans 12:11 - Not slothful in business; fervent in spirit; serving the Lord.

Jeremiah 31:25 - For I have satiated the weary soul, and I have replenished every sorrowful soul.

THE SPIRIT OF PERVERSION

The word perverse, according to merriam-webster.com, means turning away from what is right, good and proper or lacking in integrity or moral conduct. A perverse spirit works with the spirit of whoredom. Perversion is the habitual engagement of unnatural sexual practices.

All sexual sin begins with a thought. You certainly will not have victory over sexual sin, unless you take authority over the way you think. If your thoughts are not adjusted, continued deliverance will not help. The spirit of perversion can come through the reading of romance novels, watching sexually perverted movies and music videos, and entertaining lustful perverted conversations.

Sexual sin will destroy the mind, body and soul of an individual and it conditions the flesh to want to experience sex on a continual basis like food.

Manifestations

- Sexual perversion
- Having a filthy mind
- Pornography
- Chronic worrying
- Having a broken spirit
- Walking in foolishness
- Twisting the Word of God
- Doctrinal error and atheism
- Abuse
- Incest
- Evil actions
- Abortion

Scriptures to Counter Perversion

Ephesians 5:3-5 - But fornication, and all uncleanness, or covetousness, let it not be once named among you, as becometh saints; neither filthiness, nor foolish talking, nor jesting, which are not convenient: but rather giving of thanks. For this ye know, that no whoremonger, nor unclean person, nor covetous man, who is an idolater, hath any inheritance in the kingdom of Christ and of God.

Proverbs 12:8 - A man shall be commended according to his wisdom: but he that is of a perverse heart shall be despised.

Proverbs 17:20 - He that hath a froward heart findeth no good: and he that hath a perverse tongue falleth into mischief.

SPIRIT OF REJECTION

Rejection causes a severe wounding of the heart, sometimes so painful that the mind refuses to deal with it, so the individual buries it in their subconscious. Rejection is one of Satan's most effective forms of oppression. A spirit of rejection can come through the womb as a generational curse. It works alongside fear by creating an inner voice that tells the individual they are unworthy, unlovable and inferior. The truth is, we were created to be loved, accepted, and appreciated. Rejection is an anti-Christ spirit because it opposes the very nature that God created in us.

Manifestations

- Supersensitive and touchy.
- Rejection of others as a protection mechanism.

- Perfectionism.
- Emotionally immature person who becomes co-dependent on others for affirmations.
- Feeling of unworthiness.
- Harshness, hardness, skepticism, unbelief.
- Pride.
- Low self-image, inferiorities, insecurity and inadequacy.
- Feeling of unworthiness.
- Self-accusation and self-condemnation.
- Fear of failure and fear of other's opinions.
- Depression, pessimism and hopelessness and despair.
- Self-righteousness and self-justification.
- Self-idolatry, criticism, judgmental attitudes, envy, jealousy and covetousness.
- Self-pity.
- Control: someone who wants to dominate others because he/she is afraid that he/she would otherwise be hurt.
- Perfectionism: Many become perfectionists trying to prove their worth, gain love and acceptance.

THE LYING SPIRIT

A lie is saying or failing to say something with intent of creating a false belief. A lie has an intention to deceive. Proverbs 12:22 says: "Lying lips are abomination to the Lord: but they that deal truly are his delight."

Manifestations

- Accusations

- Condemnation
- Stealing and cheating
- False prophesy
- Gossip
- Guilt
- False teaching
- Religious bondages
- Self-deception and shame
- Flattery
- False memory
- False Burden
- Melancholy spirit
- Exaggeration
- Frenzied emotional action
- Slander
- Strong deception

OCTOPUS SPIRIT

The octopus spirit works in conjunction with the sins of the flesh. The head is a spirit of idolatry/witchcraft control, while the others are fleshly sins such as lust, rage, selfish-ambition or gluttony. The octopus spirit takes advantage of the weak, fleshly appetite of an individual to lead them to surrender to an addictive, destructive or obsessive behavior. Whatever destructive behavior that the individual falls into, they cannot become free unless deliverance takes place.

Manifestations

- Ungodly sexual behaviors.
- Deceived perception: believing that your situation is unique, and that specific Scriptures don't apply to you.

THE SPIRIT OF OPPRESSION/HEAVINESS

This is an evil spirit that seeks to control the different aspects of your life (mentally, physically, emotionally and spiritually). This domination or suppression will ultimately affect your ability to reach your full potential. Its oppressive tactic involves restricting your God-given human potential. This stalls God's plans for your life and crushes your spirit with a sense of being weighed down in body or mind. Long term oppression causes depression within a person, with the intent to cause regression (or people to go backwards).

Manifestations

- Weariness
- Excessive mourning
- Sorrow/grief
- Insomnia
- Bi-polar
- Manic depressive
- Self-pity
- Rejection
- Broken heart
- Despair/dejection/hopelessness

- Depression
- Confusion
- Suicidal thoughts
- The desire to die or give up
- Inner hurts/torn spirit
- Heaviness
- Sadness
- Low-self esteem
- Loneliness
- Oppression
- Discouragement
- Stress/strain
- Extreme tiredness
- Lethargy
- Deep sleep (for days possibly), spirit of abandonment

Scripture on Oppression

Psalm 9:9 - The Lord also will be a refuge for the oppressed, a refuge in times of trouble.

KUNDALINI SPIRIT

This is a demonic spirit that is a counterfeit to the Holy Spirit and is now quite popular in the church today. It masquerades as the Holy Spirit, showing works that mimic the manifestation of the Holy Spirit or pretending to support the work of God. Kundalini spirit can be transmitted through a Hindu Guru or the individual can call on the spirit himself through meditation, for example, yoga.

"For such are false apostles, deceitful workers, transforming themselves into the apostles of Christ. And no marvel; for Satan himself is transformed into an angel of light. Therefore it is no great thing if his ministers also be transformed as the ministers of righteousness; whose end shall be according to their works." (2 Corinthians 11:13-15).

"The same followed Paul and us, and cried, saying, these men are the servants of the most high God, which shew unto us the way of salvation. And this did she many days. But Paul, being grieved, turned and said to the spirit, I command thee in the name of Jesus Christ to come out of her. And he came out the same hour." (Acts 16:17-18).

Manifestations

- Uncontrollable shaking or involuntary head and body movements; weird hand movements.
- Falling down and rolling about as though drunk.
- A serpent is coiled in the spine.

PYTHON SPIRIT

A python spirit is a demonic spirit in the waters. A python is the largest snake on the face of the earth. It coils itself around the individual and chokes the breath out of its victims. It doesn't kill its victims immediately; rather, it tightens its grip gradually around its victims until they are dead. Python spirit is a territorial spirit. There are international, national and continental python spirits that reside over cities, states, counties and nations. It is a spy spirit that collects data on activities of governments, people, individuals (their purpose), ministries, about their level of anointing, missions, operations and levels of authority. These spirits report back to the kingdom of darkness in order to stall God's will. Python spirit assigns demonic spirit to track and manipulate individuals.

Manifestations

- Operates by using the individual's past against them (See Isaiah 29:4). It reminds them of their negative experiences, past sins and the individual begins to condemn him/herself. It is a voice from the past.
- Being surrounded by wrong relationships, the individual becomes easily influenced by their peers and begins to compromise their Christianity.
- It steals the persons anointing, drags the Spirit of God from them and destroys them.
- Whenever you feel like you are about to break into another dimension, it blocks your progress. You begin to feel useless, bound and fearful.

Scripture to Counter the Python Spirit

2 Samuels 22:5-6 - When the waves of death compassed me, the floods of ungodly men made me afraid; the sorrows of hell compassed me about; the snares of death prevented me.

JEZEBEL SPIRIT

This is a narcissistic, manipulative spirit. It fantasizes about having unlimited admiration, beauty, power, success and brilliance.

143

Jezebel is genderless and can operate in both men and women, with or without their knowledge. Jezebel had a daughter called Ataliah.

Manifestations

- Aims to get the man to submit to her by playing psychological games, bringing about confusion.
- A personality that wants to stay at the center of attention.
- It needs admiration; yet undermines and insults.
- Selectively spinning information or events to bring about doubt, causing bewilderment and confusion.
- Totally void of empathy to seduce and control their victims.
- Undermining and insulting someone to pull their confidence and strength and bring low self-esteem.
- Has a sense of entitlement, demands automatic compliance with its expectations, unreasonable expectations of others and is critical when disappointed.
- Exploitive, abusive, takes advantage of others to achieve its goals, manipulates and lies.
- Creates a huge distraction from God due to the web that it creates. The spirit is referred to as the black magic spider.
- Creates and thrives alongside Ahab spirit (see next spirit).
- Usually married. If single, could be lesbian, homosexual man or promiscuous man.
- Critical of others and vicious to the point of blood thirsty.

Scripture on the Jezebel Spirit

Revelation 2:20 - Notwithstanding I have a few things against thee, because thou sufferest that woman Jezebel, which calleth herself a prophetess, to teach and to seduce my servants to commit fornication, and to eat things sacrificed unto idols.

AHAB SPIRIT

This spirit is driven by lust, fear, insecurity, emasculation and has an inability to be firm.

Manifestations

- Indecisiveness. The woman will take the lead.
- Emotionally unstable.
- Gives up his authority in the home to keep the peace.
- Wants to please their spouse, who is normally a Jezebel.
- Lacking drive and passion for life.
- Consistently asking for forgiveness, even when what happened is not their fault.
- Always needing approval because of low self-esteem.

Scriptures on Ahab Spirit

1 Kings 16:30 - And Ahab the son of Omri did evil in the sight of the Lord above all that were before him.

1 Kings 21:25 - But there was none like unto Ahab, which did sell himself to work wickedness in the sight of the Lord, whom Jezebel his wife stirred up.

LEVIATHAN SPIRIT/SPIRIT OF PRIDE

Leviathan is a vast sea monster of tremendous strength, described as the most powerful and dangerous creature in the ocean. He is known as the king of pride and is a sea serpent. Leviathan is a counterfeit to the Holy Spirit; it is an anti-Christ spirit. Leviathan has seven ministries: pride, lies, murder, evil heart, mischief, false witness and chaos (See Proverbs 6:16-19). Leviathan is also called the imitator of God. One can conquer leviathan through deep humility and the believer's authority. The Bible speaks to the fact that only God's sword can destroy leviathan in Isaiah 27:1, Ezekiel 29:3-5 and Job 41:10.

Manifestations

- Spirit of pride.
- It attacks our insecurities and produces feelings of pride, insufficiencies and inadequacies.
- Creates chaos, destroys ministries, marriages, relationships, governments.
- Brings sorrow, stubbornness, idolatry, an inflexible spirit, legalism in the church, perversity and inability to respond to the Holy Spirit.
- Aggressiveness, strife, deception, intimidation, mockery.
- Doublemindedness.
- Feeling entitled, claiming rights and blaming God for bad things.
- Causes neck, shoulder and upper back pain or a very stiff neck.
- Can also cause jaw to move involuntarily.

Scriptures on Leviathan Spirit

Isaiah 27:1 - In that day the Lord with his sore and great and strong sword shall punish leviathan the piercing serpent, even leviathan that crooked serpent; and he shall slay the dragon that is in the sea.

Proverbs 21:4 - An high look, and a proud heart, and the plowing of the wicked, is sin.

Proverbs 11:2 - When pride cometh, then cometh shame: but with the lowly is wisdom.

Ezekiel 29:3-5 - Speak, and say, Thus saith the Lord God; Behold, I am against thee, Pharaoh king of Egypt, the great dragon that lieth in the midst of his rivers, which hath said, My river is mine own, and I have made it for myself. But I will put hooks in thy jaws, and I will cause the fish of thy rivers to stick unto thy scales, and I will bring thee up out of the midst of thy rivers, and all the fish of thy rivers shall stick unto thy scales. And I will leave thee thrown into the wilderness, thee and all the fish of thy rivers: thou shalt fall upon the open fields; thou shalt not be brought together, nor gathered: I have given thee for meat to the beasts of the field and to the fowls of the heaven.

THE SPIRIT OF JEALOUSY

Jealousy is a sinful emotion that leads to division, hate, and even murder. The person who is jealous concentrates on the life of another and forgets their own blessing and purpose. The spirit of jealousy causes one to be ungrateful and shows dissatisfaction for what God has given them.

Manifestations

- Revenge
- Anger/rage
- Hatred
- Murder
- Cruelty
- Strife
- Competition
- Envy

Scriptures on the Spirit of Jealousy

Numbers 5:14 - And the spirit of jealousy come upon him, and he be jealous of his wife, and she be defiled: or if the spirit of jealousy come upon him, and he be jealous of his wife, and she be not defiled.

Proverbs 6:34 - For jealousy is the rage of a man: therefore he will not spare in the day of vengeance.

Galatians 5:26 - Let us not be desirous of vain glory, provoking one another, envying one another.

SPIRIT OF HEAVINESS

This is demonic spirit that brings a heavy oppressive feeling that quenches your faith.

- It darkens our countenance: Our hearts are down cast. This spirit brings a "heaviness" over us.

- It dims our vision, robs our hope. The room may look darker.
- It may come over many at once, like a plague. It can be like a cloud, hanging over a place.
- It causes us to isolate ourselves from others. It steals our love and makes us feel alone.

Manifestations

- Excessive mourning
- Sorrow/grief
- Self-pity
- Rejection
- Broken heart
- Dejection
- Hopelessness
- Depression
- Suicidal thoughts
- Inner hurts/torn spirit

Scripture on the Spirit of Heaviness

Isaiah 61:3 - To appoint unto them that mourn in Zion, to give unto them beauty for ashes, the oil of joy for mourning, the garment of praise for the spirit of heaviness; that they might be called trees of righteousness, the planting of the Lord, that he might be glorified.

SPIRIT OF WHOREDOM

This spirit causes you to focus on the flesh and on self-gratification.

Manifestations

- Chronic dissatisfaction
- Love of money
- Fornication
- Idolatry
- Unfaithfulness
- Excessive appetite
- Worldliness

Scripture on the Spirit of Whoredom

Hosea 5:4 - They will not frame their doings to turn unto their God: for the spirit of whoredoms is in the midst of them, and they have not known the Lord.

DEAF AND DUMB SPIRIT

This is a demonic spirit that tries to render its victims ineffective by working against the mind. It attempts to close the mouth and ears to prevent its victims from learning and progressing.

Manifestations

- Suicidal
- Crying
- Tearing
- Dumb/mute
- Blindness
- Mental illness

- Ear problems
- Foaming at the mouth
- Seizures/epilepsy
- Gnashing of teeth

Scripture on Deaf and Dumb Spirit

Mark 9:24-25 - And straightway the father of the child cried out, and said with tears, Lord, I believe; help thou mine unbelief. When Jesus saw that the people came running together, he rebuked the foul spirit, saying unto him, thou dumb and deaf spirit, I charge thee, come out of him, and enter no more into him.

SPIRIT OF BONDAGE

This spirit controls and influences your actions.

Manifestations

- Fears
- Addictions (drugs, cigarettes, food, alcohol)
- Fear of death
- Captivity to Satan
- Bondage to sin
- Compulsive sin

Scripture on the Spirit of Bondage

Romans 8:15 - For ye have not received the spirit of bondage again to fear; but ye have received the Spirit of adoption, whereby we cry, Abba, Father.

SEDUCING SPIRITS

This is a dangerous and deceitful spirit that influences your mind against the things of God.

Seducing spirits are lying and deceiving spirits. When they take over people, they reverse the truth in their minds. They present things that are false as if they are truths and make them sound completely believable. They try to convince people that black is white, and white is black; that false is true and true is false; so that they can lead them astray. Before a person can put up a defense, the spirit moves in to take over.

Manifestations

- Deception
- Fascination with evil ways, objects or persons
- Hypocritical lies
- Seared conscience
- Attraction/fascination by false prophets
- Wandering from the truth

Scripture on Seducing Spirits

1 Timothy 4:1 - Now the Spirit speaketh expressly, that in the latter times some shall depart from the faith, giving heed to seducing spirits, and doctrines of devils.

ABOUT THE AUTHOR

ELLECIA CLARKE-EDWARDS is a purpose-driven, multi-gifted woman of God and Transformational Speaker. She is an Author, Entrepreneur and a Sales and Customer service Consultant with several years of Banking experience. She has a passion for human development and loves to assist people who are unclear about their life's purpose. She strongly holds the credence that success is non-negotiable, and prosperity is necessary in all areas of life.

INDEX

1. Zzzoetime@aol.com viewed on July 31, 2019
2. http://thehealingschool.org/Transformation_and_Sanctification/Sy mptoms_of_Unforgiveness/
3. https://www.oneplace.com/ministries/love-worth-finding/read/articles/root-of-bitterness-8599.html
4. https://embassymedia.com/file/1004/download?token=Ab3XEVjJ-viewed on August 17, 2019.
5. http://access-jesus.com/unforgiveness-definition-html/
6. https://emilyroselewis.org/2018/03/24/the-octopus-spirit/
7. https://www.healedpeople.com/knowledge/strongholds/23-oppression/17-freedom-from-oppression
8. http://walkingintruth.blogspot.com/2010/08/spirit-of-heaviness-and-oppression.html
9. ttps://www.riversofrevival.com/site/bibdisplay.asp?study_id=1800 03756&sec_id=180001249
10. http://www.rapturenotes.com/spiritual-and-demonic-oppression.html
11. https://spiritualwarrior2016.wordpress.com/2016/05/26/confronting -spiritual-lethargy/comment-page-1/
12. www.nairaland.com/2442596/dealing-incubus-succubus-sex-demons
13. Succubus and Incubus Spirit Explained Part 3 LeviathanSystem Review and Lesser Water Spirits-Pt 32-6/25/17-youtube

15. *https://www.wattpad.com/664696159-demonic-strongholds-completed-lying-spirit*

16. https://sermons.faithlife.com/sermons/20191-defeating-the-spirit-of-compromise

17. *web.oru.edu › current_students › class_pages › grtheo › mmankins › DrJBar (viewed in 11/17/19*

18. https://www.ernestangley.org/read/article/seducing_spirits1

19. *https://www.merriam-webster.com › dictionary › perverse*

20. Hill, Napoleon: The Law of Success, The Master Wealth Builder's Complete and Original Lesson Plan for Achieving Your Dreams, eighth volume.

21. Allen, James: As a Man Thinketh, http://www.AsAManThinketh.net

www.ingramcontent.com/pod-product-compliance
Lightning Source LLC
LaVergne TN
LVHW051639080426

835511LV00016B/2396